湖北省学术著作
Hubei Special Funds for
Academic Publications
出版专项资金

龙山文化玉记
The Longshan Cultural Jade Records

中华新石器时期玉记丛书
The Series of Neolithic Jade Records of China

杨天佑　　程龙保　编著

武汉理工大学出版社

内容简介

本系列丛书的书名为《中华新石器时期玉记丛书》,共有《红山文化玉记》《良渚文化玉记》《龙山文化玉记》与《黑皮玉及其文字》四个分册,系统地介绍了新石器时期的玉文化。它属于文物考古范畴,既是一部记载了重要的史前文物遗存的考古文献,也是一部中华新石器时期玉器雕塑艺术作品的汇总典籍。众多精美玉器展现了中华祖先在新石器时期所创造的辉煌。

玉器是中华新石器时期的重要文化载体,它们形象地展现了中华新石器时期的社会面貌。根据这些玉器的造型,作者对当时中华大地上的氏族源流、宗教信仰、文化传承、社会性质及其演变、人们的生产和生活方式、主要的社会问题、不同文化区系间的文化交流等做了深入的探讨和分析,因此本书具有重要的文物价值、考古价值和艺术价值。

本系列丛书所选用的玉器以新石器时期的红山文化、良渚文化和龙山文化三大玉文化发达区的玉器为主体,兼有其他文化区的玉器,因为这三大区系的玉器所提供的文化信息足以反映新石器时期中华玉文化的特征,其他地区的玉文化基本上是这三大文化区系玉文化的扩散。新石器时期的玉文化是泛红山玉文化的继承和延续,本丛书第四册介绍了属于泛红山文化玉器的一百余件黑皮玉,这部分黑皮玉的共同特点是每件玉器上雕刻有文字,这表明泛红山文化的文明层次很高,也显示新石器时期玉器有很深的文化底蕴。

图书在版编目(CIP)数据

龙山文化玉记 / 杨天佑, 程龙保编著. —武汉 : 武汉理工大学出版社, 2017.8
（中华新石器时期玉记丛书）
ISBN 978-7-5629-5611-2

Ⅰ. ①龙…　Ⅱ. ①杨…　②程…　Ⅲ. ①龙山文化—古玉器—研究
Ⅳ. ①K876.84

中国版本图书馆 CIP 数据核字(2017)第 210790 号

项目负责人 : 王兆国　　　　　责任编辑 : 王兆国
责 任 校 对 : 徐　环　　　　　装帧设计 : 许伶俐
出 版 发 行 : 武汉理工大学出版社
网　　　　址 : http://www.wutp.com.cn
地　　　　址 : 武汉市洪山区珞狮路 122 号
邮　　　　编 : 430070
印　　　　刷 : 武汉中远印务有限公司
发　　　　行 : 各地新华书店
开　　　　本 : 787×1092　　1/16
印　　　　张 : 9
字　　　　数 : 230 千字
版　　　　次 : 2018 年 1 月第 1 版
印　　　　次 : 2018 年 1 月第 1 次印刷
定　　　　价 : 166.00 元

前　　言

　　龙山文化分布地域较广，主要在中国东部沿海地区，包括山东、江苏与河北等沿海地区及辽东半岛一带。最初于 1928 年发现位于山东省章丘县龙山镇的城子崖遗址，故以"龙山文化"称之，时间距今约 4400 年至 3900 年前。其他地区的龙山文化有湖北龙山文化，黄河中游地区的龙山文化(包括河南龙山文化、陕西龙山文化与山西襄汾陶寺文化等)。这些地区的龙山文化与东部沿海地区的龙山文化时间相近，且同处于相同的发展阶段，故考古学界将它们统归于龙山文化。以上的龙山文化遗址均有玉器出土，但以山东龙山文化玉器及与其有相同文化性质的湖北龙山文化中的石家河文化玉器最为称著。因此，本分册所选用的玉器也以此为重点。新石器时期山东地区的考古文化序列为北辛文化—大汶口文化—龙山文化—岳石文化。其时间约是距今 7700 年至 3600 年前，即有 4000 多年的发展历程。其玉文化自大汶口文化时期就很发达。本分册中也选用了若干件大汶口文化玉器以至更早的北辛文化玉器。山东龙山文化区介于东北的红山文化区与江南的良渚文化区之间，其玉器造型明显受到南北两方面影响。如钩云形佩、方圆形璧、璇玑、环形龙、鹰等造型均受到红山文化的影响，而玉琮、梯形佩、兽面图腾像等则受到良渚文化的影响。这种影响是与氏族迁徙直接相关的。山东龙山文化区的主要氏族是东夷族，但东夷族中有很多分支，如鹰为少昊族图腾，牛、羊为羌族图腾，猪为豕韦氏图腾。东夷族中的主要氏族是太昊、少昊族，其他氏族多为他们的分支。新石器时期早期即有豕韦氏与羌族迁入山东地区，并且加入了太昊、少昊氏族联盟，图腾的造型可以证明这一点。早期从西北迁入的羌族对该地区制陶工艺的发展起了推动作用。本书选用的玉制礼仪器中即有炎帝像、炎帝氏族的连山符及炎帝世系的夸父族图腾像。新石器时期晚期至夏代初期又有部分羌族自山东回迁至西北和四川成都平原,他们又将山东龙山文化的制玉传统带到了上述地区(参看《巴蜀玉缘》一书,浙江大学出版社,2008,杨天佑著)。豕韦氏也是山东地区的重要氏族。自北辛文化时期至龙山文化时期此地均有以猪头或猪下颚骨随葬的习俗,并且从墓葬的发掘证明当时很多人有凿齿的习俗,且以獐牙作为装饰。《良渚文化玉记》前言中曾讲到豕韦氏与凿齿氏属同一族群。他们源自末次冰期的泛红山文化时期,在新石器时期他们的分布很广,包括山东的大汶口—龙山文化区、良渚文化区及湖北龙山文化区等地。他们的后裔直到商周时期还是望族。本书选用了几件西周时凿齿氏的领袖像,以证实其源流关系。自新石器时期晚期至商代不断有凿齿氏向海外迁徙,主要是澳洲和南美洲,这些地区有许多凿齿氏的遗迹。他们对南美洲奥尔梅克文明的创建有过重要的贡献。总之,凿齿氏是新石器时期的一个重要氏族,他们对中华文明与美洲文明的创建均有过重大的贡献。在龙山文化系列中,本书还选用了几件河南龙山文化、陕西龙山文化及二里头文化玉器。这些玉器多为兵器形的礼仪器,均属新石器时期晚期五帝时期的玉作。

本书中还列举了几件江淮地区文化玉器,其中包括北阴阳营文化玉器、凌家滩文化玉器等。其时间均比龙山文化区系早,多数在距今5000年前左右。玉器的品类以璜、玦、珠等女性佩饰居多,表明这些地区尚处于母系社会阶段。本书的一件北阴阳营七孔玉刀,体量大,制作精致,十分罕见。另一件凌家滩型玉人是女性,与1987年出土于凌家滩的一件玉人风格相似,但工艺不同,此件的制作不是以阴刻为主,而是以磨制为主,具有泛红山文化玉作的特点,应属该地区较早的玉作。凌家滩地区出土了很多玉器,且独具风格。从其玉器的造型与氏族图腾的造型可知,该文化区的玉文化仍是泛红山玉文化的沿袭。因为其图腾造型主要有野猪、龟、鹰、龙等,而这些动物均为泛红山文化时期的重要图腾,也是新石器时期红山文化区、山东龙山文化区和良渚文化区等地氏族的图腾,其中有些与泛红山文化玉作形状相似,如环形龙、龟壳、展翅鹰等。凌家滩玉人与牛河梁出土的红山文化玉人形状也极相似。特别是其中最大的一件,重达88千克的玉猪,其造型和工艺均与泛红山文化玉作相似(《红山文化玉记》图1.63)。前文已讲到,野猪是豕韦氏图腾,该氏族在红山文化、龙山文化与良渚文化中均扮演重要角色。这件玉猪表明豕韦氏也是凌家滩地区的文明开创者之一。

本书还选用了两件卑南文化玉器,即《红山文化玉记》图1.26与本书图3.67,它们是东夷族中的畎夷即犬封族的图腾造型。在总论中已经提到过,泛红山文化时期犬封族生活在东南沿海地区,新石器时期他们一部分生活在台湾,是卑南文化的创建者;还有一部分迁往甘肃,辛店文化即是犬封氏文化。商周时期的犬戎族即是他们的后裔。《红山文化玉记》图1.26是一件泛红山文化时期犬封氏图腾造型。

　　总之，龙山文化时期是新石器时期的重要阶段，这一时期大多数文化区系均已由母系社会转化为父系社会，政权性质也由氏族公社转化为中央集权。该时期的玉器形制也相应地由以原始宗教信仰为主体转化为王权与巫权合一，即政教合一的形制。这一时期的玉器中出现了很多象征王权的兵器类造型。这一时期即是五帝时代，也即是楚国学者风胡子所说的玉兵时代。

　　本书的玉器可分为四部分：第一部分是人物造像与氏族图腾，第二部分是礼器，第三部分是其他类型的龙山文化玉器，第四部分是其他地区的新石器时期文化玉器。

Preface

There was a wide geographical distribution of Longshan culture, mainly distributed in the eastern coastal areas and Liaodong Peninsula area. Longshan culture was first discovered in 1928 in Longshan site, Zhangqiu County, Shandong Province, so named after Longshan culture. It was about 4400—3900 years ago. Other Longshan cultural areas cover Hubei Longshan cultural district and the mid-reaches of the Yellow River, including Henan Longshan cultural district, Shaanxi Longshan cultural district and Shanxi Taosi cultural district. The time of these cultures were close to Longshan culture in eastern coastal region, and at the same stage of development, so archeologists attributed them to Longshan culture. There were unearthed jade pieces at all of the cultural sites mentioned above; the most famous sites were Shandong Longshan cultural sites and Hubei Shijiahe Longshan cultural sites. Therefore, the jade works chosen in this book are focused on these regions. Shandong archaeological cultural series during the Neolithic period is Beixin culture—Dawenkou culture—Longshan culture—Yueshi culture, which is about 7700—3600 years ago, and its developmental course has gone through more than 4000 years. Since Dawenkou cultural period, its jade-making was very well developed. A number of Dawenkou cultural jade works as well as the former Beixin cultural jade works have been selected in this book. The Longshan cultural district located between northeast Hongshan cultural district and south Liangzhu cultural district, and its jade types obviously were influenced by the cultures both north and south. For example, cloud-shaped ware, square-round Bi, Xuanji (a ring with convex teeth), ring-shaped dragon, eagle, etc. were influenced by Hongshan culture; and Cong, trapezoidal-shaped ware, animal mask, etc. were influenced by Liangzhu culture. These effects were directly related to the clan's migration. In this region, the main clans were Dongyi nationality, of which the Taihao, Shaohao family were the main clan, and many of their branches there. During the early Neolithic period, the Shiwei and Qiang people moved into Shandong area, and joined the Taihao and Shaohao Clan alliances. For this, it can be proved by the modeling of clan's totem. The Qiang people, who moved from Northwest of China in early time, played a role in promoting the development of the ceramic technology of this region. There are some ritual devices in this volume; we can see some important pieces among them, such as the Emperor Yan image, the chain-mountain symbol of Emperor Yan, and the leader's image of Kuafu Clan which was an important branch of Emperor Yan Clan. From the late Neolithic period to the early Xia Dynasty, some of Qiang people from Shandong moved to the Northwest China and Western Sichuan plain, so the jade-making tradition of Shandong Longshan culture was brought to these areas. The Shiwei Clan was an important clan in Shandong region. From Beixin culture period to Longshan culture period, they had a special burial custom of putting pig skull or pig mandible bone in the tomb. Another discovery of their custom was to pull out the canines and decorate with the sharp animal teeth. That is the Zaochi's special custom; and it is the source of the clan's name—Zaochi Clan. As mentioned in the preface of *The Liangzhu Cultural Jade Record*, the Shiwei Clan and the Zaochi Clan were the same clan. Since the Last Glacial, they were active clans in Northeast Asia. During the Neolithic period, they were d istributed over vast areas, including Shandong Longshan cultural district, Liangzhu cultural district and Hubei Longshan cultural district and other areas. Until the Shang and Zhou Dynasties their descendants still were a prominent family. In this book, we chose a few pieces of the leader's images of Zaochi Clan in Western Zhou Dynasty to confirm the relationship with its origins. From the Neolithic period to the Shang Dynasty, Zaochi Clan often immigrated overseas. There are many cultural remains of them in Australia and South America. In short, Zaochi family was an important clan in the Neolithic period. They had a great contribution to the Chinese civilization and American civilization. We also selected some of the Henan Longshan cultural jade, Shaanxi Longshan cultural jade and Erlitou cultural jade in this book, most of which are ritual devices in the weapon's shape. All of them were made in Five Emperors period during the late Neolithic period.

In this book, we also listed some jade pieces of Jianghuai cultural District, which include the Beiyinyangying cultural district and Lingjiatan cultural district. The time of these cultures is earlier than Longshan culture; the majority of them are 5000 years ago or so. Most of the categories belong to woman's accessories, such as rings, slotted rings, Huang pieces, beads and so on; it shows that it was still in the stage of matriarchal society of this region. There is a Beiyinyangying jade knife with seven holes in this book, which had a large body and was well-made, very rare. Another one is a jade woman image, which is similar to the one unearthed in this area in 1987, but the process is different. It is in the Pan-Hongshan cultural jade style, which should belong to the earlier jade in this region. A number of jade pieces were discovered in Lingjiatan archaeological excavations. From their shapes and the images of clan's totem, we can see that Lingjiatan culture also followed Pan-Hongshan culture. Because most of their totem's shapes are boar, turtle eagle, dragon, etc., and these animals were important clan's totems during the Pan-Hongshan cultural period, and also they were the clan's totems in the Hongshan culture area, Shandong Longshan cultural area and Liangzhu cultural area, and some of their jade shapes were similar to Pan-Hongshan cultural jade, such as dragon ring, turtle shell, eagle and human image, etc.. In particular, there is a jade pig weighting 88 kg, whose shape and technology were similar to the Pan-Hongshan cultural jade (refer to *The Hongshan Cultural Jade Record*, Figure 1.63). As mentioned earlier, pig is Shiwei's totem; this clan played an important role in the Hongshan culture, Longshan culture and Liangzhu culture during the Neolithic period. This jade pig indicated that Shiwei Clan also was one of the pioneers of creating Lingjiatan culture.

We also selected two pieces of the Beinan cultural jade (Figures 1.26 in the book *The Hongshan Cultural Jade Record* and Figure 3.67 in this book), both of which are the totemic images of the Quanfeng's people. We have mentioned them in the General Remarks that the Quanfeng Clan was a branch of Dongyi; the dog is their clan's totem. During the Pan-Hongshan cultural period, they lived in southeast coast areas. A part of them lived in Taiwan during the Neolithic period, and they were the creators of the Beinan culture; another part of them migrated to Gansu area and they were the creators of Xindian Culture during the Neolithic period. Their descendants were still active in the Shang and Zhou Dynasties. The jade piece showed in Figure 1.26 in *The Hongshan Cultural Jade Record* belongs to the Pan-Hongshan cultural jade work.

In short, the Longshan culture period was an important stage of the Neolithic period. During this period, most of the cultural districts were transformed from matriarchal society to patriarchal society, and the nature of regime also transformed from the clan's commune to the centralization. The jade shapes were correspondingly changed. In this period, many weapon-shaped jade works representing the royal power occurred. This period is the Five Emperors period, which is the "Jade Weapon's Era" mentioned by the Chu scholar Fenghuzi.

The jade pieces in this book can be divided into four parts: the first part is human figures and clan's totems; the second part is the three dimensional ritual devices; the third part is other types of jade pieces of Longshan culture; the fourth part is the Neolithic cultural jade pieces in other cultural regions.

目录

Contents

新石器时期玉文化总论

（1）艰难创业的时代

末次冰期结束时，由于地球暖化，冰川迅速消融，海水猛涨。在距今 10700 年前左右，海平面猛涨 50 米，大面积沿海陆地和海岛沉入海底，太平洋面积增加一倍左右。自然环境和生态环境均发生了极大变化，很多物种在灾难中消失。此次灾难同样是灭绝人种的灾难，只有极少数人类在灾难后存活下来。人类即是在这样悲惨的情况下进入了冰后期，地质年代表上称作"全新世"，即新石器时期。新石器时期早期，即距今 10000 年前至 8000 年前左右，末次冰期晚期的灾难余波未平，地震、洪水、海啸、干旱等自然灾难不断，人类仍面临着极其艰难的生存环境。古史传说中的女娲补天、精卫填海、羿射九日等皆是这一时期的故事，表明当时人们经历了严酷的山崩、地裂、洪水、干旱等灾情，并与其做不屈不挠的斗争，顽强地存活了下来。

在灾难中，随着自然环境与生态环境的变化，人类被迫向适合生存的地方迁徙。如中国东部沿海地区由于海侵，大面积陆地被淹没，生存空间锐减，迫使沿海居民（主要是东夷族群）向内陆迁徙。在此期间，内陆地区居民也因气候环境极不稳定，冷暖干湿变化无常而迁徙。如在甘青高原的古羌族地区，因气温的变化，雪线随之变化，引发洪水和旱灾，因此古羌人也向东部和南部地区迁徙。总之，人们是从自然环境恶劣的地区向适合生存的地方迁徙。这样在某些地区即会形成人口比较密集的氏族部落群，促进了不同族群间的文化交流，进而发展成为新石器时期文化发达地区，并在中华大地上逐渐形成了若干个文化中心地带，如黄河流域文明、长江流域文明、黑龙江流域文明等。在距今 8000 年前至 4000 年前的这段时间里，中华大地上如群星闪烁，展现出一派生机勃勃的多元的文化景观。这一时期即是新石器时期的繁荣期。在此期间，人们的物质文明和精神文明均得以快速发展。新石器时期晚期已进入铜石并用时代,社会组织也逐渐由氏族公社、氏族联盟向中央集权发展,并出现了军队,已经是国家的形态。这一时期即是五帝时期。

新石器时期晚期,距今大约4100年前至4000年前,适逢宇宙期,又发生了一次世界性的水患灾难。中国东部沿海地区和中原地区均长年遭受洪涝灾害,造成大量人畜伤亡,人们在新石器时期创建的文明遭到严重破坏。此次洪灾虽没有末次冰期结束时的灾难大,但由于发生于人口密集区,人员伤亡量大,其时间又在尧、舜、禹时期,已接近夏代,故留给人们深刻的印象。

总之,新石器时期是人类历史上的一个辉煌时期。它从巨大的自然灾难中开始,又在巨大的自然灾难中结束。这个时期人们不畏艰苦、勇于开创,是创建人类文明的重要时期,当时的英雄人物与神奇悲壮的传说已成为人们永久的记忆。

(2)新石器时期是人类文明的重要历史阶段

一般认为,新石器时期有三大文化特征,即磨制石器的发明、陶器的发明与农业的产生。其实,这三大特征在晚更新世后期曾经出现并发展到相当高的水平。与中华大地新石器时期文化直接相关的即是源自东北亚并扩散至环太平洋地区的泛红山文化,该文化始自末次冰期晚期,毁灭于末次冰期结束时的大灾难中(参看杨天佑《万古奇珍——泛红山文化玉群》一书)。泛红山文化时期的诸文化因素,除了上述三项外还有很多,如畜牧业、渔业、航海业、天文、医药卫生、手工业,特别是制玉发展到相当高的水平,且该时期已经是文明社会。虽然这一文明在巨大的自然灾难中消失,但劫后余生的极少数人类不同于晚期智人,他们是有着文明背景的新人。他们的智力与对环境的适应能力远远超出晚期智人,在新石器时期他们继承并沿袭了泛红山文化的若干文明因素,这就是他们为什么能在长期艰难的环境中生存,并且迅速创建新一轮文明的原因。世界其他地区也有类似的情形。因此,新石器时期在世界范围内呈现出旧石器时期人类不可比拟的飞跃发展与进步,迅速向文明迈进。所以,新石器时期是承前启后、开创人类文明的重要时期。

(3)玉文化是中华新石器时期特有的文化特征

除了上述新石器时期三大特征外,中华新石器文化还有一个重要特征即是玉文化。新石器时期中华大地上很多重要的考古文化都有玉文化。从地域上看,东北地区和沿海地区玉文化尤为发达。这显然与末次冰期的泛红山文化有关,因为上述地区恰是泛红山文化的分布区与扩散区,而玉文化是泛红山文化的重要特征,且各类新石器文化玉器的造型几乎均源自泛红山文化玉器。从族群上看,新石器时期黄帝族与东夷族均有悠久的制玉传统,他们的祖先轩辕氏、有熊氏、伏羲氏、女娲氏、少昊氏、豕韦氏、蚩尤氏、后夔氏等在泛红山文化时期都是善于制玉的氏族,新石器时期他们的分布地域主要是现在的中国东北部与东南沿海地区,因此,新石器时期玉文化呈现出自东向西扩展的态势。新石器时期,中华大地上不同的玉文化发达区系在玉器的材质、造型、纹饰及加工手段上均有明显差异,但是以玉美化生活、以玉作为通灵宝物、以玉代表权势则是共同的。特别应该重视的一点即是玉文化自末次冰期的泛红山文化时期开始即是与原始宗教中各种原始崇拜密切相关的,当时人们将玉作为人神沟通的媒介物。所以,玉文化自其开始就与石文化、陶文化不同,玉器常常是作为礼器、祭器与装饰器,即使作为实用器也常是权势的象征,因此玉文化属于精神文明的范畴。凡是玉文化发达的史前考古文化,其文明层次都是比较高的。如新石器时期的红山文化、良渚文化、龙山文化均以玉文化著称,它们的文明层次都是比较高的。

新石器时期,不同文化区系的玉文化也有广泛的交流。近年来,很多学者将不同文化区系的玉器从材质、造型与工艺手段上加以比较,从玉文化的角度研究不同文化区系间的文化传播和交流,有了很多重要的发现。总体看来,玉文化的传播,早期(即自末次冰期至新石器时期早中期)自北向南形成了东部沿海地区的一个新月形的玉文化分布区,晚期(即从新石器时期晚期至夏代)则是东部地区的玉文化向西部扩散。如前文所述,中国的东北及东北亚地区是玉文化的源头,新石器时期各文化区系的玉文化有其同源性。但由于不同文化区系的族群、宗教信仰、生产和生活方式等的差异,其玉文化也各有其特点,在中华大地上呈现出一派多彩多姿的玉文化的繁荣景象,这即是新石器时期玉文化的繁荣期,时间大约是距今6000年前至4000年前。这是中华文明史上的一个重要的历史时期,这一时期繁荣的玉文化大大加速了中华文明的发展进程,并且使玉文化成为贯穿中华文明始终的文明因素、中华民族特有的文化基因。众多的史前玉器是史前文明极其重要的文化载体,是我们打开史前文明大门的钥匙。

（4）关于泛红山文化

在末次冰期晚期，人类曾经有过一次文明的高峰期。在东北亚地区，出现了以泛红山文化为代表的史前超文明。它在末次冰期结束时遭到了毁灭，但其中一部分文明因素延续到了新石器时期。这一文明是与中华文明及环太平洋地区文明密切相关的，又与中国北方地区的红山文化关系更为直接，即中国北方的红山文化及时空范围更为广泛的红山诸文化都是它的部分继承与延续，故笔者以"泛红山文化"命名。这一文明虽遭毁灭，但其一部分文明因素仍保留了下来，其中主要是玉文化。大批的泛红山文化玉器遗存再现了泛红山文化时期曾经有过的辉煌，这一批玉器笔者称之为"泛红山文化玉群"。该玉群以其恢宏的气势、高超的艺术水平与工艺技巧向世人展示了一幅具有深广文化内涵的史前超文明画面，它是人类史前文明的一大奇观，是世界人类文化宝库中的重要遗存。该玉群向人们提供了许多泛红山文化时期重要的文化信息。这些信息是我们研究考古、历史、人类、生态、艺术、雕塑，以及现代人类起源等课题极为重要的素材。

红山文化是新石器时期中国北方具有代表性的考古文化，并且以玉文化著称，是新石器时期中华玉文化的重要源头。红山文化及与其性质相似的中国北方的红山诸文化均属于泛红山文化范畴，它们是新石器时期的泛红山文化。红山文化的各类玉器造型均被涵括于泛红山文化玉群中，这表明了它们之间的继承关系，本丛书第一册选用了一百余幅泛红山文化玉器，显示了泛红山文化在史前文明中的地位与作用。另外，本丛书第四册选用了一百多件黑皮玉，它们也是与红山文化玉器直接相关的一部分泛红山文化玉器。黑皮玉发现于泛红山文化时期的一个高水平的祭祀中心，其时间约为距今14000年前，地处现在的内蒙古地区，那里有很多大型的玉器，特别是很多玉器上雕刻有文字，显示当时那里已有很高的文明层次，那里的人们已进入文明社会，同时也反映了红山文化和新石器时期的玉文化都有着很深的文化底蕴。

（5）族群迁徙与玉文化的发展态势

前文提到，新石器时期是中华大地上多氏族大迁徙、大融合的时期，其间包括了氏族的战争、联合、吞并等，逐渐形成了中华大地上几个强大的氏族，即华夏族、东夷族与苗蛮族。这一过程持续到夏代，华夏族已成为中华大地上的主体氏族。新石器时期的早中期，善于制玉的黄帝族与东夷族多分布于现在的中国东北与东南沿海地区,故自现在的中国东北至东南沿海地区形成了一个新月形的玉文化发达区,其中包括红山文化、山东龙山文化、良渚文化、北阴阳营文化、凌家滩文化、卑南文化、石峡文化等。至新石器时期的中晚期,中华大地上形成了一个玉文化的繁荣期,玉文化扩展到了现在中国的中西部地区,如河南龙山文化、湖北龙山文化、陕西龙山文化、齐家文化、陶寺文化、神木石峁文化等。有些学者称这一时期为中华玉器时代,笔者认为称此时期为新石器时期的玉文化繁荣期比较合适,因为真正的玉器时代是新石器时期之前的泛红山文化时期。

上述玉文化繁荣期的形成时间与中国古史传说中的五帝时代是相合的。为方便理解五帝时代玉文化的发展,有必要将这一时期中华大地上氏族迁徙与融合的过程简述如下:首先,应明确黄帝族与东夷族是善于制玉的氏族,他们在距今10000年前的泛红山文化时期即是如此。那时黄帝族是轩辕氏与有熊氏的联合氏族,是后来华夏族的前身。另外,从龙、鸟等图腾造型看,他们与东夷族很早以前即有亲缘关系。黄帝族与东夷族是末次冰期玉文化的开创者,又是新石器时期玉文化的继承者与推广者。新石器时期早期,黄帝族主要分布于现在的中国华北与内蒙古等地,东夷族主要分布于东部沿海地区。根据史书记载,黄帝在涿鹿战胜蚩尤,又在板泉战胜炎帝,其势力由北向南延伸到中原地区黄河流域一带,并与黄河流域炎帝神农氏的氐羌族融合为华夏族,后又与东夷族联合,其势日盛,征战频频,势力范围不断向四方扩充。正如《史记·黄帝本纪》所载:"东至于海,登丸山,及岱宗;西至于崆峒,登鸡头;南至于江,登熊湘;北逐荤粥,合符釜山,而邑于涿鹿之际。"黄帝时代自此而始。历史上的五帝皆属黄帝氏族。五帝第一位为黄帝,第二位为颛顼(高阳氏),第三位为帝俊,又名帝喾(高辛氏),第四位为帝尧,第五位为帝舜。颛顼时,帝都由涿鹿迁往帝丘(今河南濮阳市),帝俊时又迁到亳(今河南偃师市),可见黄帝势力逐渐深入到中原地区。帝尧是帝俊的次子,名放勋,号陶唐氏,是一位贤能的领袖,他迁都到平阳(今山西临汾市),这对兼有南北诸文化因素的陶寺文化(距今4600年前至4000年前)的形成起了推进作用。另外,新石器时期晚期,颛顼母系的一支名为蜀山氏,自山东迁往蜀地,他们也将山东龙山文化的制玉传统带到了黄河上游地区和川西平原。这时华夏族已成为黄河流域的主要氏族了。五帝时期处于由母系社会向父系社会过渡的阶段,在政体上处于由氏族联盟向中央集权过渡的时期。新石器时期晚期,中原地区与良渚文化区等地已出现了具有王国性质的中央集权制。五帝时以华夏族与东夷族的联盟为主体,例如舜即是东夷族人。

五帝时期,华夏族曾与分布于长江中下游的三苗、九黎、古越等族有过长时期的战争。这一地区是稻作农业发展最早的地区,文明程度很高。如江浙一带在黄帝时即是上述族群的聚居区,也即良渚先民的聚居地。他们有相当发达的农业与手工业,特别是高水平的制玉技能。他们较早地进入了父系社会,在新石器时期晚期已发展到王国阶段。自黄帝与蚩尤战后,他们与华夏族的征战从未停息,如舜即是死于与三苗征战途中的苍梧,葬于九疑,即零陵(今湖南宁远县)。直到舜、禹之时,长江中下游地区发生特大洪水,将该地区的文明毁灭殆尽,三苗族无力与华夏族征战,遂向南方和长江中上游地区以至黄河上游地区迁徙,良渚玉文化也随之扩散,如广东的石峡文化遗址、江汉地区的石家河文化遗址、四川广汉地区的三星堆文化遗址、山西陶寺文化遗址、甘青地区的齐家文化遗址等都有良渚文化型玉器出土就是证明。禹在治理洪水后,即平定了三苗。禹死后葬于会稽(今浙江绍兴)。当然,长达数百年的战争也促进了氏族间的融合。近年来,中国基因普查结果表明,汉族与苗族的基因最接近,其历史原因即是氏族融合。回顾了上述一段历史,即可使我们了解为什么新石器时期中晚期中华玉文化会有如前文所述的发展态势。

(6)新石器时期玉文化的发展历程

如前所述,新石器时期是人类历史上承前启后的时期,对于中华玉文化而言也是如此。这里所谓承前,是指继承了新石器时期之前泛红山文化时期的玉文化。虽然只是部分的继承,但新石器时期自始至终玉文化并未间断。新石器时期初期,由于人口稀少,生存环境艰难,没有大规模制玉的可能,所以玉文化的发展是很缓慢的。直到新石器时期的中晚期,即距今6000年前至4000年前期间,由于农业发展,人口增加,生活相对安定,在中华大地上逐渐形成了以三大河流域为中心的文化区系,此时玉文化才得以迅速发展,出现了玉文化的繁荣期。那么,新石器时期早期,即距今大约10000年至6000年期间,玉文化何以得到延续呢?这主要归功于原始宗教,因为自末次冰期晚期至新石器时期,原始宗教始终以玉作为人与神沟通的媒介物。原始宗教在祭祀中所用的礼器、祭器在可能的情况下总是以玉制作。新石器时期早期,原始宗教可能掌握一些泛红山文化早期的玉器遗存,并且有些巫觋掌握了制玉的技艺,他们将这些技艺代代相传,故玉文化得以延续和不断发展,以至出现了很多超越当时生产力水平的制玉技巧和精美玉作,令人叹为观止。从新石器时期早中期的玉器品类看,多数是与原始宗教相关的礼仪器和美化生活的佩饰器。新石器时期晚期,随着原始氏族社会的瓦解和王权的产生,玉器的形式也产生了相应的变化,即出现了象征王权的玉器,如斧、钺、圭、璋等。特别是黄帝开创的五帝时代,出现了大批兵器形式的玉礼器,如刀、剑、斧、钺、戈、戚等,并且逐渐成为中原地区玉文化的主流。如山东龙山文化、河南龙山文化、陕西龙山文化、山西襄汾陶寺文化、二里头文化、齐家文化、神木石峁文化以至早期的广汉文化等皆是如此。这既是氏族公社向中央集权转化时期玉器的特点,也是巫权向王权的转化时期玉器的特点。这一时期玉器制作的开片技术有了长足的进步,出现了许多大体型的片状玉器,如刀、钺、圭、璋等,这些玉器体量大,开片薄且均匀,这与新石器时期晚期使用铜制工具有关。春秋时楚国风胡子所讲"黄帝之时,以玉为兵",指的即是这一时期。这一时期有关原始崇拜的礼仪器及美化生活的装饰器仍占有相当的比重,应该是巫王一体的政教合一时期。

新石器时期,中华大地上不同的玉文化发达区系,虽各有特点,但是它们又有其同源性,并且有着较长玉文化历史的玉文化发达区发展历程大致相似,即它们都经历了自以原始宗教各类礼仪器、装饰器为主体的巫玉阶段过渡到以王权为主体的王玉与巫玉并存的转化阶段。如海岱地区的北辛—大汶口—龙山—岳石文化区系及江南地区的河姆渡—马家浜—崧泽—良渚文化区系,它们都有三千年以上的玉文化史,从玉器形制上都反映了上述特点。但是北方的红山文化玉器似乎并未反映上述特点,其原因在于红山文化的时间较早,尚处于五帝时期之前,它的玉作保留了较多母系社会时期原始宗教的特点。但从其墓葬形式可知它已进入等级社会,也有权力集中的氏族首领或大巫,可以说已进入了王国阶段,只是不以斧、钺等为权力的象征,而以斜口形王冠、权杖、云形佩和玉龙等为王权的象征。

(7)新石器时期与原始宗教相关玉器型制的特点

新石器时期各个不同的玉文化发达区系的玉器造型均有明显的继承性,因为它们同是源于泛红山文化。它们的继承性主要体现在原始宗教中的各种信仰与崇拜。当然这种继承不是一成不变的,各文化区系的玉作在不同时期又各有其特点。

新石器时期的玉文化与原始宗教是密不可分的。虽然不同文化区系族群的不同、信仰的差异及时间的早晚，均会反映到玉文化上来，但是以玉作为通灵神物、护身的宝物，以玉作为人神之间的媒介，以玉通神、以玉为礼则是共同的。或者说，它们都有"巫—玉—神"这个统一的玉文化模式。即使到了原始氏族公社向王权转化的时期，原始宗教并未被削弱，只是巫与王合为一体了，王即是大巫。

总体看来，新石器时期的玉器关系到原始宗教的各个方面，如自然崇拜、灵魂崇拜、祖先崇拜、图腾崇拜、生殖崇拜与性崇拜等。泛红山文化玉群中独具特色的外星生命体崇拜在新石器时期玉器中也有体现。在各种原始崇拜中尤以图腾崇拜与生殖崇拜表现突出。这是因为图腾是氏族的共同生命体象征，图腾崇拜始终是氏族社会原始宗教的主要内容。又因为末次冰期结束时的灾难对人类来说是毁灭性的，新石器时期的人口问题已经是关系到人类是否能延续的重大问题，所以生殖崇拜及与其直接相关的性崇拜在原始宗教中占有突出的地位，同时也成为新石器时期玉文化贯穿始终的主题。

新石器时期的先民们对大自然是充满信仰与崇拜的，因为大自然是他们赖以生存的环境与条件。前文中提到，末次冰期结束时的灾难及新石器时期初期严酷的自然环境，令先民们经历了长期艰难动荡的生活历程，给人类留下了深刻的记忆，因此，他们将天、地、山、川、湖、海、风、雨、雷、电等均视为威力强大的神灵，对它们无不充满敬畏之情，并且认为自然界的万物皆是有灵性的。在新石器时期的考古研究中，有关自然崇拜的发现屡见不鲜，如原始岩画、石器、陶器、玉器等均有与自然崇拜相关的形象，如丛书第一册的图 1.29 即是雷神的造型。有些氏族图腾的造型也是与自然崇拜相关的，如第一册中的云形佩等。

灵魂崇拜也是原始宗教的重要内容。灵魂崇拜即是认为人的灵魂可以脱离肉体而单独存在。死人的灵魂即是鬼魂。人死后，一定要入土安葬，举行葬礼后灵魂才能安定，再次托生成人或者升天。因此，灵魂崇拜的表现是各种不同的葬俗。正因为如此，远古时期的各种墓葬为今人了解当时人们的生活习俗提供了许多实物见证，它们是人文考古的重要信息源，有人称之为"无字地书"。以玉随葬是中华民族特有的葬俗。如红山文化区系中，原氏族领袖的墓葬是积石冢的形式，且以玉随葬；良渚文化区系中，王者的墓葬为高台墓地，也有大量的玉器随葬。因为人们认为玉是最有灵性的媒介物，可以帮助死者的灵魂飞升或转世。在以玉随葬的墓中，各种玉器除了表示死者的身份、权势与财产之外，均有使死者灵魂飞升或转世的寓意。

　　新石器时期，有关祖先崇拜的人物造像玉作并不多见。至今发现的新石器时期玉制的人物造像几乎都是泛红山文化的直接继承，如大汶口文化的人物面像、陕西龙山文化的人物头像、山东龙山文化的凿齿氏面像、石家河文化中头戴折角帽的东夷族头像、凌家滩人物造像、卑南文化中的人物造像等均可在泛红山文化玉群中找到它们的原型。

　　泛红山文化时期尚处于母系社会，母祖的造型较多。新石器时期早中期，母祖造型也很多，但多是陶制或泥制的作品，其中最有名的当属辽西牛河梁女神庙中陶塑母祖群像及泥塑女神像。另外，仰韶文化中半坡型、庙底沟型陶器也都有母祖形象。马家窑文化的一件母祖形彩陶壶也颇有名。限于当时制玉水平，玉制的母祖形象很少见。新石器时期晚期，很多文化区系已进入父系社会，并进入玉文化的繁荣期，制玉水平提高，所以出现了一批男性氏族领袖的玉雕像，如红山文化、良渚文化、山东龙山文化、湖北龙山文化等均有制作水平较高的这类雕像。

　　在新石器时期，祖先崇拜常是与生殖崇拜互相联系的，如母祖的造型常常是孕妇的形象；而"男祖"的称谓即是指男性生殖器。威严的男性祖先像常常有性图腾标识或其本身即是性图腾的形象，这也是泛红山文化的传承。这一习俗沿袭很久，如东汉山东嘉祥武梁祠画像石上的中华始祖伏羲与女娲的造型即是生殖之神的形象，乃至今日河南淮阳人祖庙会上的泥塑女娲造型也是生殖之神的形象。

　　新石器时期，图腾崇拜的内容也多是泛红山文化的继承，玉制的各类图腾造型多出现于新石器时期中晚期。新石器时期早中期各类图腾形象多出现于陶器的纹饰上。这些图腾形象表明了自末次冰期至新石器时期与这些图腾相关氏族的延续性。新石器时期很多动物图腾被赋予或加强了生殖崇拜、性崇拜的内涵。如红山文化玉猪龙是豕韦氏的图腾，同时也是男性的图腾，从其出土的数量可知，它是红山文化时期普遍的图腾造型。另外，鸟图腾造型在各个玉文化发达区，如红山文化、龙山文化、良渚文化中数量都很大，这除了表明以鸟为图腾的氏族较多外，也有男性的寓意。同样，鱼、蛙等图腾也有女性的寓意。新石器时期晚期，很多文化区系转向父系社会，如龙山文化区、良渚文化区等。这些地区的图腾祖先造像与氏族领袖造像也常与男性图腾整合为一体。

　　生殖文化与性文化在泛红山文化时期即是原始宗教中的重要内容。与之相关的精美玉器尚有留存（第一分册图 1.87—图 1.94 及第二分册图 2.7—图 2.10）。

总体来看,新石器时期的生殖文化与性文化玉作还是泛红山文化的延续,但也有其明显的时代特点,主要表现如下:

1. 以简单的几何造型表示男女性别。如以圆形或半圆形的璧、环、玦、璜等表示女性;以珠、管等表示女阴;以方形、梯形、山字形等表示男性。

2. 以某些动物图腾表示性别。如以龙、虎、鸟、野猪等表示男性;以鱼、蛙等表示女性。

3. 以符号表示性别或生殖器。如以方代表男,圆代表女;正反两个"6"字组合形表示男根;以卵形目纹或多重回纹表示睾丸;以牛角、羊角表示男性雄风等。

4. 新石器时期祖先崇拜与图腾崇拜的造型中时常融入生殖崇拜与性崇拜的寓意。

上述特点在红山文化、龙山文化与良渚文化中表现得尤为突出。相关的玉器在本丛书中均可见到。

在此顺便讲一下带有缺口的环形玦。这是一种非常古老的产生于母系社会的玉器,其分布地域很广。从目前玉玦出土的情况看,其产生的源头应是距今10000年以前的泛红山文化时期的东北亚地区,其后逐渐沿中国海域扩散到中国大陆东南沿海地区、台湾地区,以及东南亚诸国、韩国、日本等地。考古发掘证实,玦都出土于女性墓地。以玉随葬的应是氏族的权贵人物,故玦应是有权势女性的表征。如卑南文化中,有一件头戴图腾标志的玉人,其头部即是玦形,表明她是该氏族的女性领袖(参看《中国玉器全集1》,图301)。本丛书中有一件与其相似的头戴图腾标志的玉人(第三册图3.67),但其头部是环形,表明该玉人应是男性氏族首领。另外, 第一册图 1.26 也是一件类似的泛红山文化玉人,其头部是玦形,胸部是两并列玉环,表示一对丰满的乳房,并体现出女体的形象,更明确地表示她是一位女性的领袖或母祖。从河姆渡—马家浜—崧泽—良渚文化系列可明显地看出玦的文化表征。河姆渡、马家浜、崧泽文化时期尚处于母系社会,故玦的出土量所占比例很高,至良渚文化时期,已是父系社会,在王者的大墓中随葬的玉器以象征王权的钺、琮、璧等为主,而玦几乎是销声匿迹了。玦的形状并不单一,但时间最早、出土量最大、分布地域最广的玦是带有缺口的环形玦。笔者认为这种玦有女性子宫的寓意。其后又出现了许多其他形状的玦,早期它们都是女性的象征物或是女性的佩饰物。玦不一定是耳饰,有些玦上还有供穿戴用的孔,如很多卑南文化玉玦都有孔,本丛书中的一件良渚文化玉玦(第二册图2.121)也有一对孔,可供穿戴。玦形玉器延续很久,直到春秋战国时期,甚至秦汉时期还很流行,但已失去了女权或女性饰物的原义,成为男女均可佩戴的饰物,并赋予它不同的含义。在此不赘述。

新石器时期,原始宗教中仍然继承了泛红山文化时期对外星生命体的崇拜习俗。外星人的造型及不同类动物融合体的造型在新石器时期比较少见,而新石器时期晚期却出现了外星飞行器的造型,这一变化为我们提供了重要的文化信息。红山文化玉器中的猪龙、C形龙、Y形器等,实际上都是不同类动物的融合造型,属泛红山文化玉器范畴。此类玉器也出现在其他的考古文化中,特别是良渚文化中的兽面纹,它是泛红山文化玉器中外星生命形象的直接继承。良渚兽面纹是良渚文化区原始宗教的主图腾,几乎在各类良渚文化玉器上均可见到其形象。它是良渚先民的氏族图腾,也是男性图腾。神兽目纹也有太阳的寓意,在神兽双目之间常有一拱形或折角形连桥,它表示天穹盖。并且,此神兽面纹也常与鸟图腾组合在一起,寓意它是从天外而来,特别是第二册图2.35的造型是将此鸟兽组合图腾装饰在一个以凸内缘玉璧表示的外星飞行器上,更为良渚文化增添了几分神秘色彩。仔细观察可知,该兽面纹的双目与红山文化玉猪龙的双目几乎是相同的。笔者在《万古奇珍——泛红山文化玉群》一书中提到,良渚文化的神兽纹图腾是泛红山文化的继承,并指出玉猪龙不仅仅是某一氏族的图腾。玉猪龙的形象源自野猪,它是豕韦氏的图腾,后来发展为宇宙间普遍的灵物和保护神,也有男性图腾的含义。因此,进入父系社会的良渚先民选择它作为良渚文化区各氏族的共同族徽的主要部分,以求得良渚文化区的平安与兴旺。

良渚文化中期阶段,氏族的联盟体制已过渡到权力相对集中的王权政体。因此,在早期族徽中的兽面纹和鸟图腾之间加入了威严王者的形象,也似一个身饰鸟、兽标志的巫与王一体的形象,其轮廓像是一个"皇"字。它既是联合氏族的图腾,又是男性的图腾。其整体形象似一展翅飞翔的大鸟,不仅有羽冠、鸟足,四肢也做展翅飞翔状,表明它是自天外来的使者,即将王权神化了。同样,山东龙山文化中有几件玉圭上的纹饰与良渚文化神徽也有相同的寓意,即将氏族图腾、男性图腾与神化了的王者形象整合为一。

新石器时期的中晚期均出现了凸内缘玉璧,即内缘高于玉璧表面的璧,似两个圆形的碟子扣在一起。这种玉璧一直延续到商代。广汉三星堆出土了很多这类玉器造型。笔者认为,这类玉璧是较典型的外星飞行器(UFO)的造型。另外,有些红山文化型玉璧,即边缘减薄玉璧也有此含义。书中除了上述的一类良渚文化凸内缘玉璧外,还有龙山文化型的方圆形凸内缘玉璧(图3.47),以及两件在玉璧外缘饰有羽人的出廓璧（第三分册图 3.45、图 3.46）。这即是以玉璧表示外星飞行器，以羽人表示天外来客。这种以玉璧表示外星飞行器有一定的写实成分，而以羽人表示天外来客也是始自泛红山文化时期。在泛红山文化玉器中，这种羽人并不罕见（第一分册图 1.33），并且这种艺术造型在中国传承很久，如汉代玉器中的羽人，佛教艺术中的飞天、妙音鸟等比比皆是。

　　总之，新石器时期是人类历史上一个极为重要的时期，是承前启后、创建人类新一轮文明的时期。泛红山文化是中华文明及中华玉文化的源头。虽然泛红山文化在末次冰期结束时遭到毁灭，只有部分文明因素沿袭到新石器时期，但是这个文化沿袭对新石器时期中华大地上人类的生存与发展是有决定性意义的。中华玉文化是中华民族特有的文化。在没有文字记载的史前时期尤其突显出其重要性。特别是新石器时期的中晚期，中华大地上出现了玉文化的繁荣期，玉文化在很多地区出现了蓬勃发展的态势。众多新石器时期的玉器为后人提供了大量当时的文明信息。如果我们正确解读出这些信息，将得到一部相当完整并且以艺术形式表现的、生动的新石器时期中华文明史。本丛书名为《中华新石器时期玉记丛书》，其意即是中华民族在新石器时期以玉石记录的开创史。

General Remarks on Neolithic Jade Culture

(1) Difficult Era of Genesis

At the end of the last glacial, about 10700 years ago, due to the global warming, glaciers were melting rapidly, and so the sea surged, and sea levels quickly rose about 50 meters, so that a large area of coastal land and islands sunk, and the area of the Pacific Ocean approximately doubled. Natural environment and ecological environment had undergone tremendous changes. Many species disappeared in the disaster. The disaster is also the disaster of extinct races; only a very small number of humans survived. Mankind was in such a tragic circumstance in the beginning of the postglacial period （i.e. the Neolithic period）. During the early Neolithic period, about 10000 to 8000 years ago, the last glacial disaster still had powerful reverberations, earthquakes, floods, tsunamis, droughts and other natural disasters continued to keep a very difficult environment for man to live. Ancient Chinese legends such as the story of Nvwa fixing the sky, Jingwei filling the sea, Yi shooting the nine suns, are the stories of this period. These stories show that people have made arduous struggle with nature and tenaciously survived.

The natural environment and ecological environment changing forced human to move to a more suitable places to live. E.g. a large area in eastern coastal China was inundated, living space plummeted, and it forced coastal residents, such as Dongyi, to the inland immigration. In the meantime, residents of inland moved frequently because of unstable climatic conditions. E.g. in Gansu-Qinghai Plateau, the snow line changing caused by temperature variation led to floods and droughts, so the ancient Qiang tribe who lived in this region moved to other areas. In short, people moved from worse natural environment to suitable living areas. This would form densely populated tribal groups in some areas and promote cultural exchanging among different ethnic groups. In the meantime, a number of progressive cultural centers emerged in the land of China, such as the Yellow River Civilization, the

Yangtze River Civilization and the Heilongjiang River Civilization. During the period from 8000 to 4000 years ago, a landscape of vibrant multi-culture centers showed as blinking stars on the Chinese territory. This period is the period of the prosperity of the Neolithic period. During this period, both of the material and spiritual civilization developed rapidly. The late Neolithic Age had transited to the period of copper with stone. Society organization had changed gradually from clan corporation and clan alliance to centralization. Then the army was established and a new form of state emerged. This period was the Five Emperors Era.

During the late Neolithic period, about 4100 to 4000 years ago, coincided with the period of the Universe, a global flood disaster occurred again. The inland and eastern coastal areas in China had been flooding for years resulting in a large number of human and livestock death, and the civilization which people created in the Neolithic Age was seriously damaged. Although this disaster was not as serious as the disaster of the end of the Last Glacial, it occurred in densely populated areas in the Yao, Shun and Yu period close to the Xia Dynasty, and caused heavy casualties, so it had left a deep impression on people.

In short, the Neolithic period was a glorious period in human history. Both of its beginning and ending were in huge disasters. At that time, people had the courage to create despite difficulties; it was an important creative period of human civilization. The heroes and tragic magic legends about that time have become a permanent memory.

(2) The Neolithic Period was an Important Historical Period of Human Civilization

It is generally believed that the Neolithic culture had three characteristics, namely, the invention of polished stone tools, the invention of pottery and the emergence of agriculture. In fact, these three cultural characteristics had emerged in the late Pleistocene and developed to a very high level. The culture which directly related to the Neolithic culture of China was the Pan-Hongshan culture, which originated in Northeast Asia and spread around the Pacific Ocean; it rose in the late Last Glacial, and was destroyed during the major disaster in the end of the Last Glacial. Among the various cultural factors of Pan-Hongshan culture other than the three items mentioned above, there were many others, such as animal husbandry, fisheries, maritime industry, astronomy, medicine health and handcrafts, especially jade craft had developed to a very high level. This historic period had been developed to civil society. Although this civilization disappeared in a huge natural disaster, the surviving humans were different from the Homo sapiens, they were modern humans with background of civilization, and their intelligence and ability to adapt to the environment were far ahead of Homo sapiens. They inherited and extended a number of the factors of civilization of Pan-Hongshan culture, so this is why they could survive in long-term difficult environment and create a new civilization. Similar situations also appeared in other parts of the world. So the Neolithic period is an important historical period of human civilization. During this period, people inherited the past human civilization and opened up a new round of human civilization.

(3) Jade Culture is a Unique Cultural Characteristic of Chinese Culture in the Neolithic Period

In addition to the three features of the Neolithic culture in general, an important feature of Chinese Neolithic culture was the jade culture. The jade culture existed in many important Chinese Neolithic cultural districts. From the geographical point of view, the earlier jade cultural districts were distributed in the Northeast and the coastal areas of China. It was obviously related to the Pan-Hongshan culture of the Last Glacial, since these regions were the distribution and spread area of Pan-Hongshan culture and the jade culture was its outstanding cultural feature, and various types of Chinese Neolithic cultural jade works almost inherited from the Pan-Hongshan cultural jade works. From the ethnic point of view, in the Neolithic period, Xuanyuan tribe, Youxiong tribe, Fuxi tribe, Nvwa tribe, Shaohao tribe, Shiwei tribe, Chiyou tribe, Houkui tribe and so on, all of these tribes were excellent in jade craft, and most of them were located in the areas mentioned above. Therefore, Chinese Neolithic jade culture showed the developing trend from eastern area to western area. The differences of Chinese Neolithic jade culture in different developed areas were obvious, because the jade material, shape, decoration and processing methods in different areas were different. But using jade to beautify life, using jade as a link between god and people, and using jade on behalf of power were common. Particular emphasis is that since Pan-Hongshan culture period, jade culture was closely related to all kinds of primitive worship of original religion. Jade culture from its beginning was different from the stone culture and the pottery culture. Jade works were often used for rituals, ceremonial vessels and decorative devices, or the representation of power. Therefore, the jade culture belonged to the category of spiritual civilization. The prehistoric archaeological culture which had developed jade culture was a civilization of relatively high level. E.g. the Hongshan culture, Liangzhu culture and Longshan culture were famous for jade culture in the Neolithic period, and their civilization was also of a relatively high level.

Neolithic jade culture in different culture areas had extensive exchanges. In recent years, many scholars compared the prehistoric jade works of different cultural areas from the perspective of jade culture, studied the cultural exchanges among them, and made many important discoveries. Overall, the development status of jade culture in China is as follows: since the last glacial to the early and middle Neolithic period, the development status was from north to south and east coast area which formed a crescent-shaped distribution; during the late Neolithic period to the Xia Dynasty, the development status was from east to west. As mentioned earlier, Northeast China and Northeast Asia were the source of jade culture; Neolithic jade culture in all areas had their common source. However, because the ethnic groups in different areas had different religion beliefs, modes of production and life styles, jade culture had their own characteristics, thus a colorful landscape of jade culture occurred in the land of China. This period was the prosperous period of Neolithic jade culture; it was 6000 to 4000 years ago. It was a very important historic period of Chinese civilization. During this period, the jade culture had greatly accelerated the process of Chinese civilization, and made jade culture run through the entire history of Chinese civilization and become Chinese cultural gene. A large number of prehistoric cultural jade pieces were important cultural carrier and the key to open the gate of prehistoric civilization.

(4) About Pan-Hongshan Culture

In the Last Glacial, we human beings had a relative peak of civilization. In Northeast Asia a prehistoric super-civilization occurred being represented by Pan-Hongshan culture. It had been destroyed in the end of the Last Glacial, but part of its civilized elements extended to the Neolithic period. This civilization is closely related to Chinese civilization and the civilization of Pacific Rim, especially more directly related to the Hongshan culture and Neolithic cultures in North China. These Chinese Neolithic cultures were the partial inheritance and continuity of Pan-Hongshan culture. This is why we called this prehistoric super-civilization "Pan-Hongshan culture". The most important remain of Pan-Hongshan culture was its jade culture. The large number of Pan-Hongshan jade remains once again showed the brilliant period of that era. With the magnificent momentums, the superb art and craftsmanship, as well as the broad and deep cultural connotation, the jade group showed people a picture of the prehistoric super-civilization. It was a great human wonder of the prehistoric civilization and an important relic of human culture. The jade group had provided us with much important information of the Pan-Hongshan culture period; these are extremely important materials for us to study archaeology, history, ecology, art, sculpture and such subjects of the origin of modern people.

Hongshan culture was the representative Neolithic archaeological culture in North China. It was one of the sources of Chinese jade culture in the Neolithic period. Hongshan culture and all similar archaeological cultures in North China belonged to the scope of Pan-Hongshan culture; they were Neolithic Pan-Hongshan cultures. All kinds of Hongshan cultural jade were encompassed in the jade group of Pan-Hongshan culture; this indicated the inherited relation between them. More than one hundred pieces of Pan-Hongshan cultural jade are chosen in Volume I, and they have shown the position and role of Pan-Hongshan culture in the prehistoric civilization. In addition, one hundred more black-shell jade pieces are chosen in Volume IV, which are also directly related to Hongshan cultural jade works. Black-shell jade works were found in a high-level Pan-Hongshan cultural worship center, which is about 14000 years ago, and the location is in Inner Mongolia region, where there are many large jade works, especially a lot of jade engraved writing characters, which shows a high cultural level there at that time, and people had entered a civilized society at this region. As well, it reflects Hongshan culture and Neolithic jade culture have their deep cultural heritage.

(5) Clan Migration and Developing Trend of Jade Culture

As previously mentioned, the Neolithic period is a period of great migration and large integration of Chinese clans. During this period, there were clan wars, associations, annexations, etc., gradually forming a few powerful clans, namely Huaxia, Dongyi and Miaoman. This process continued until the Xia Dynasty, and Huaxia had become the main clan in China. During the early and middle Neolithic period, Emperor Huang and Dongyi, who excelled at jade craft, settled in northeast and southeast coast of China, and formed a geographical crescent of developed areas of jade culture, including Hongshan culture, Shandong Longshan culture, Liangzhu culture, Beiyinyangying culture, Lingjiatan culture, Beinan culture, Shixia culture, etc. During the middle and late Neolithic period, the prosperous era of jade culture had formed in the land of China, and jade culture extended to China's central and western regions, such as Henan Longshan cultural area, Shaanxi Longshan cultural area, Hubei Longshan cultural area, Taosi cultural area, Shenmu Shimao cultural area, etc. Some scholars called this period "Chinese Jade Age", but I believe that to call this period "prosperous era of jade culture" is more appropriate, because the real jade age was in Pan-Hongshan culture before the Neolithic period.

The time of the prosperity of jade culture mentioned above and the time of China's ancient Five Emperors were consistent. In order to facilitate the understanding of the development of jade culture in Five Emperors Era, it is necessary to give an outline of the ethnic migration and integration process during this period. First of all, it should be clear that during the Pan-Hongshan culture era 10000 years ago, both of Emperor Huang tribe and Dongyi tribe excelled at jade craft. At that time, the Emperor Huang tribe was a united clan which was formed by the combination of the two clans, Xuanyuan and Youxiong. They were the later Huaxia. From the totem's shape such as dragon, bird, etc., we know that Emperor Huang tribe and Dongyi tribe were relatives for a long time. They were the founders of jade culture in the Last Glacial and also the successors and promoters in the Neolithic period. Early Emperor Huang people were mainly distributed in North China and Inner Mongolia, Dongyi mainly in the east coastal area. According to historical records, Emperor Huang defeated Chiyou in Zhuolu, and defeated Emperor Yan in Banquan, whose influence expanded to the Central Plains from north to south, and allied with the Diqiang people, who lived in the Yellow River valley together formed Huaxia nation, and also allied with Dongyi. Their power became increasingly strong, and continued to expand to outlying areas. Historical records of their geographical areas are as follows: East to the East China Sea Coast , Wan Mountain and Tai Mountain; west to Kongtong and Jitou Mountain; south to Yangtze River, Xiong Mountain and Xiang Mountain; in north, Emperor Huang's united clan forces defeated the ethnic Xunyu, and joined forces in the Fu Mountain, and then established capital in Zhuolu. Emperor Huang era began. All of the Five Emperors belonged to the Emperor Huang's family. The first one of the Five Emperors was Emperor Huang, the second was Zhuanxu (Gaoyang), the third was Emperor Jun or Emperor Ku (Gaoxin), the fourth was Emperor Yao, and the fifth was Emperor Shun. During the Zhuanxu period, the capital had been moved from Zhuolu to Diqiu (now Puyang City in Henan Province), and during Emperor Jun period, moved to Bo (now Yanshi City in Henan Province). Thus, it can be seen that the Emperor Huang's power gradually expanded into the Central Plains. Yao was the second son of Emperor Jun, whose name is Fangxun, and family name is Taotang, and he was a wise and competent leader. During the Yao period, the capital was moved to Pingyang (now Linfen City in Shanxi Province), and it played a catalytic role for the formation of Taosi culture which had various cultural factors of both north and south China. In addition, during the late Neolithic period, one of the Zhuanxu's matrilineal branches named Shushan moved from Shandong to Sichuan, and they brought the traditional jade craft of Shandong Longshan culture into the upper reaches of the Yellow River and West Sichuan Plain. For this time, Huaxia had become the major clan of the Yellow River Basin. The Five Emperors period was a transitional period from the matriarchal society to the patriarchal society; and it was the regime transitional period from the clan alliances to the centralized system. During the late Neolithic period, in the Central Plains and the Liangzhu cultural district, the kingdoms with the nature of the centralized system had appeared. During the Five Emperors period, the union of the Huaxia and Dongyi was the main form of government. For example, Shun was a Dongyi people.

During the Five Emperors period, Huaxia waged a long war with the Sanmiao and Jiuli, etc. which distributed in the middle and lower reaches of the Yangtze River, whose regions was the earliest development area of rice cultivation. There had been high level of civilization. Such as Jiangsu and Zhejiang regions were inhabited by Liangzhu ancestors, who had well-developed agriculture and hand crafts, especially high-level skills in jade works. They had entered into a patriarchal society, and in the late Neolithic period they had entered the kingdom. Since the time that Emperor Huang defeated Chiyou, they never stopped the war with Huaxia. For example, Shun died on the way to the war with Sanmiao in Cangwu, and he was buried in Lingling (now Ningyuan County in Hunan Province). During the Shun and Yu period, a big flood occurred in the middle and lower reaches of the Yangtze River, and the Liangzhu civilization in this area had been exhausted and destroyed. Sanmiao had been unable to fight with Huaxia, so they had to move to other areas, such as Guang-dong and the middle and upper reaches of the Yangtze

River, Liangzhu jade culture also had spread to these vast areas. Since the last century, many Liangzhu cultural jades have been found in various cultural sites, such as the Shixia site in Guangdong, Shijiahe site in Hubei, Sanxingdui site in Sichuan Guanghan, Taosi site in Shanxi, Qijia site in Gansu and Qinghai regions and so on. After the flood was controlled, Yu had occupied Sanmiao; he was buried in Kuaiji (now Shaoxing City in Zhejian Province). Of course, centuries of war also contributed to the integration of the clans. In recent years, survey results showed that the genes of Han and Miao were close; its historical reason was the result of the integration of the clans. Recalling the history above, it would enable us to understand why during the middle and late Neolithic period, jade culture had the developing trend shown above.

(6) Development Process of Jade Culture during the Neolithic Period

As mentioned earlier, during the Neolithic period, people inherited some former civilization factors and opened up a new round of human civilization; for Chinese jade culture it was the same. The Neolithic jade culture inherited a part of the Pan-Hongshan jade culture of the Last Glacial. Although it had been only the part of the inheritance, the jade culture never stopped throughout the Neolithic period. In the early Neolithic period, because of population decrease and difficult living conditions, there was no possibility of making a large number of jade works, so the jade culture development was very slow. During the middle and late Neolithic period (6000 to 4000 years ago), due to the population increase and the agricultural development, people's life was relatively stable, so in the land of China some cultural districts which concentrated in the three rivers (Yellow River, Yangtze River and Heilongjiang River) had gradually formed. At this time, the jade culture was able to develop quickly, and the jade cultural prosperity emerged. However, how did the earlier Neolithic jade culture develop? This was mainly due to the primitive religions, because those religions had always served with jade as the communication media between people and God. The jade productions were in possible use for the ritual and ceremonial vessels in primitive religions. During the early Neolithic period, the primitive religions may have some remains of Pan-Hongshan cultural jade relics and skills of jade crafts, and they transferred their skills from generation to generation, so jade culture could continue and develop. It makes people amazing for many skills and exquisite jade works beyond the level of production at that time. From jade category of the early and middle Neolithic period of view, most of them were associated with primitive religion's rituals and accessories. During the late Neolithic period, with the collapse of the clan's commune and the emergence of royal power, there was also a corresponding change in the form of jade works; some of the symbol of royal power jade works had occurred, such as axe, Yue, Gui, Zhang, etc. In particular, during the Five Emperors period, a large number of weapon-shaped ritual jades had emerged, such as knives, swords, axes, Yue, Ge, Qi, etc., and gradually become the mainstream of jade culture in Central Plains, including many cultural regions, such as Shandong Long-shan culture, Henan Longshan culture, Shaanxi Longshan culture, Shanxi Xiangfen Taosi culture, Erlitou culture, Qijia culture, Shenmu Shimao culture, Guanghan culture and so on. These had reflected the jade cultural characteristics during the conversion period from the clan commune to the centralized government, or from the wizard's power to the royal power. During this period, the jade slicing techniques had made great progress, and many large size of sheet-shaped jade works emerged, such as knives, Yue, Gui, Zhang, etc. These jade pieces are in large size, thin and uniform thickness, which was related to the use of copper tools in the late Neolithic period. In the Spring and Autumn Period, Chu scholar Fenghuzi once said that: "During the Emperor Huang period, the weapons had been made with jade". The Emperor Huang period that he referred to was the conversion period. During the conversion period, the ritual jade and accessory jade related to primitive religions were still a considerable proportion of jade works. During this period, the wizard and the king, as well as the religion and the politics had combined into one.

During the Neolithic period, the jade cultures in different cultural regions had their own characteristics, but they were homologous, and had a similar process of development in those culture regions which had a long history of jade culture. Generally, they had gone through two stages. The first was the wizard jade stage; the second was the coexisting stage of wizard jade and royal jade. During the first stage, the jade making was based on all kinds of primitive religion rituals and accessories; during the second stage, the jade making was based on the jade representing the royal power. E.g. Beixin-Dawenkou-Longshan-Yueshi cultural system in Haidai area; and Hemudu-Majiabang-Songze-Liangzhu cultural system in the lower reaches of the Yangtze

River. Both of them had long history of jade culture of more than 3000 years, and the evolution of jade shapes in these areas reflected the characteristics mentioned above. Hongshan culture retained the more primitive religious characteristics of matriarchal society. It had entered a hierarchical society, and also had the concentration of power in the clan leader or a great wizard. In fact, it had entered ancient kingdom. Judging by the type of its jade works, they don't have axe, Yue, etc., as a symbol of power, but with crown, mace, cloud-shaped pendant, jade dragon and so on as a symbol of royal power.

(7) Neolithic Jade Characteristics Associated with Primitive Religion

During the Neolithic period, there was apparent inheritance of jade shapes in each developed jade cultural area. The common source of these cultures was Pan-Hongshan culture. Their inheritance was mainly reflected in all kinds of primitive worships in the original religion. Of course, such inheritance was not static; the jade production had its own characteristics in different cultural districts and different times.

During the Neolithic period, jade culture and primitive religion were inseparable. Although in different culture regions, there were many differences, such as different clans, different religious beliefs, different times and so on, all of which would be reflected in jade culture, the concepts of jade as psychic religious artifacts, as the truly inspired ritual, and the medium between people and God were common. Or that they had a uniform "wizard-jade-God" model of jade culture. Even in the period of transformation from clan commune to monarchy, the original religion had not been weakening, but wizard and king had combined into one, and the king was a great wizard.

Overall, Neolithic jade culture is associated with all aspects of primitive religion, such as nature worship, soul worship, ancestor worship, reproductive worship, sexual worship; and the unique worship of alien life was also reflected in the Neolithic jade culture. Among them the most important was the totem worship and reproductive worship. This is because the clan totem was a common form of life; totem worship was always the main element of primitive religion. And because the disaster in the end of last glacial was devastating to humans, only very few people survived after the disaster, so the population problem had been the very important problem, which is related to the continuation of human race. Therefore, the reproductive worship had occupied a prominent position in the original religion. Also they had become the consistent theme in the Neolithic jade culture.

During the Neolithic period, people were full of reverence for nature, because nature was the environment and necessary conditions for survival. As mentioned before, because of the disaster of the last glacial and the early Neolithic harsh environment, people have experienced a long-term turbulent and difficult process of life. This left a deep memory on people. Therefore, people were all filled with awe to heaven, earth, mountain, sea, wind, rain, thunder, lighting, etc., and thought of all things in nature as spiritual. At that time, people imagined wind, rain, thunder, electricity and other natural phenomena as powerful gods to worship, such as Greek legends of the god of wing—Aeolus, the god of thunder—Raytheon and so on. There also was the image of the thunder god in the Pan-Hongshan jade group (Volume Ⅰ Figure 1.29). In the Neolithic archaeological discoveries, the nature worship was common; they were discovered in rock art, stone tools, pottery and jade works and so on. Some of the jade of the nature worship was in the form of clan totem, such as the cloud-shaped pendants among the Pan-Hongshan cultural jade group.

The soul worship was an important part of original religion. The view point of soul worship was that the human soul could exist in separation from the body; the soul is ghost of the dead. After death, people must be buried and holding funeral meant to make the soul calm, to rebirth or to go to heaven. Therefore, the performance of the soul worship contained all kinds of funeral customs, and because of these customs, people today could understand the ancient life through the ancient tombs. The various ancient tombs are important sources of information for archeology. Some scholars called them "No words ground book". Jade burial was the specific burial custom of Chinese nation. For example, in the Hongshan cultural area, the clan leader's tombs had been made of stone and put jade inside; in the Liangzhu cultural area, the king's tombs were built on a small hill and put many jade in it. As the ancient people considered, jade is the spiritual medium, and it could help the deceased's soul to go to heaven or to rebirth. The morals of the jade burial practices were helping the deceased's soul to go to heaven or to rebirth other than the meaning for the identity, property and power of the deceased.

During the Neolithic period, the jade figure statues related to the ancestor worship were rare. So far, all of Neolithic jade figure statues have been discovered, which were almost the direct successor of the Pan-Hongshan cultural jade. For example, the facial figure of Dawenkou culture and Shaanxi

Longshan Culture, the Zaochi's faces of Shandong Longshan Culture, the Dongyi statues of Shijiahe Culture, the figure statues of Lingjiatan Culture, the figure statues of Beinan Culture, etc. All of them could be found their prototypes in Pan-Hongshan cultural jade group.

As the society during Pan-Hongshan culture period was matriarchal, there were many female ancestors' figures in Pan-Hongshan cultural jade group. In the early and middle Neolithic period, there were also many figure statues of female ancestors, but most of them were made of pottery or clay. One of the most famous was undoubtedly the Goddess Temple and the female ancestor statue's group in Niuheliang site, west of Liaoning Province. In addition, the female ancestral images were discovered in the Banpo, Yangshao cultural sites and Miaodigou, Yangshao cultural sites, and a Majiayao cultural pottery pot with female ancestor's decorating was also famous. At that time, being limited to the level of jade making, jade human statues were rare. In the late Neolithic period, many cultural districts entered into the patriarchal society and the prosperous period of jade culture, the level of jade making had been raised and some of male clan leader's jade statues appeared. In many cultural areas, such statues with higher artistic level had been produced, such as Hongshan culture, Liangzhu culture, Shandong Longshan culture, Hubei Longshan culture and so on.

In the Neolithic period, ancestor worship and reproductive worship were often interrelated. E.g. the shapes of female ancestors were often the images of pregnant women, while the title of "male ancestor" was referred to male genital. Majestic male leaders often wore the symbol of a sexual totem, or they were the image of a sexual totem, which was the Pan-Hongshan cultural inheritance, and these customs were followed for a long time. E.g. some statues of Fuxi and Nvwa were the images of the reproductive totem in the Eastern Han Dynasty. Even today, some Nvwa's statues are still in the form of a reproductive totem.

In the Neolithic period, the contents of the totem worship mostly inherited the Pan-Hongshan culture. Many types of jade totem had appeared in the middle and late Neolithic period. In the early and middle Neolithic period, the types of totem images mostly appeared in the decorative patterns on pottery. These totemic images showed that the continuity of the clans which were related to these totems extended from the Last Glacial to the Neolithic period. In the Neolithic period, many animal-shaped totems had been given or strengthened the morals of the reproductive and sexual worship. E.g. the Hongshan cultural jade pig-dragon was the Shiwei's totem and also the male totem. In addition, there were many bird-shaped images in the developed jade cultural areas; bird-shaped totem had a male implication too. Similar to the bird totems, the fishes, frogs, etc. symbolized female. During the late Neolithic period, many cultural areas transited to the patriarchal society, and in these areas, the clan's totem or the clan leader's statue often integrated with male totem.

During the Pan-Hongshan culture period, the reproductive and sexual culture was an important part of original religion; some of the fine jade pieces which were made in that time still remained (Volume Ⅰ Figures 1.87— 1.94, Volume Ⅱ Figures 2.7—2.10). Overall, during the Neolithic period, the jade related to the reproductive and sexual cultures were a continuation of Pan-Hongshan jade culture, but they had their distinctive features of the times. The important findings were as follows:

1. They put the gender or genital of male or female in simple geometric shapes. Such as the circular or semicircular Bi, rings, Jue pieces (slotted rings), Huang pieces, etc. stand for women, and beads, tubes, etc. stand for vulva; square, trapezoidal, trident shape, etc. stand for the male.

2. They put the gender of male or female in animal-shaped totems. Such as dragons, tigers, birds, boars, etc. stand for males; and fishes, frogs, etc. stand for females.

3. They put sex or genital in symbols. Such as to put male genital in a symbol of the combination of normal and reverse "6"; to put the testis in egg pattern or spiral pattern; to put horns stand for the strong masculinity.

4. As mentioned above, the ancestor worship was often integrated with the reproductive worship or sexual worship.

The characteristics mentioned above had been very prominent in Hongshan culture, Liangzhu culture and Longshan culture. The jade pictures related to these features can be seen in this series of books.

By the way, we talk about the ornament Jue, a slotted ring. This was a very old jade shape emerged in the matriarchal society. It had a very wide geographical distribution. In the view of current unearthed situation, the source of Jue was Northeast Asia, and it occurred was 10000 years ago, during the Pan-Hongshan culture period. Then it had gradually spread to the southeast coast of China, Taiwan, Southeast Asia, Korea, Japan, etc. The archaeological excavation had confirmed that all of Jue were unearthed in female cemeteries. The owner of the tomb with jade burial must have been a rich and powerful leader or nobility in the clan before her death. For example, in the Beinan cultural area, a jade female statue was unearthed; her head was in a Jueshape that showed her being a female clan leader (*The Complete Works of Chinese Jade , Volume 1*, Figure 301). There's a similar jade human statue in this book (Volume Ⅲ Figure 3.67), whose head was in a ringshape, and it should be a statue of male clan leader . In Beinan culture, the ring-shape could represent male. There's another similar female statue in Beinan cultural style in this book, which is a Pan-Hongshan cultural jade piece (Volume Ⅰ Figure 1.26). The Hemudu-Majiabang- Songze-Liangzhu cultural series showed clearly their cultural characteristics.The Hemudu, Majiabang and Songze cultural periods were still in the matriarchal society, so jade Jue pieces were greater in quantity in the excavation; but the Liangzhu cultural period was in patriarchal society, in the great royal tombs, the main types of jade were in weapon styles, and Jue pieces almost disappeared. The shapes of Jue were not single, but the earliest, the largest unearthed and the most widespread Jue was in the shape of slotted ring with a gap. This kind of Jue symbolized a women's uterus. The early Jue pieces were symbols of female or women's accessories. Jue was not necessarily earrings; it could also be the pendant of necklace. As Figure 2.121 in Volume Ⅱ shows, because of a pair of perforations in the Jue, it can be used to wear as a pendant. Jade Jue continued for a long time, until the Warring States period, as well as the Qin and Han Dynasties it was still popular, but lost the original meaning of women's power and accessories, and was given to other meanings,which we do not discuss here.

The primitive religion of the Neolithic period still inherited the worship of the living body of external space of Pan-Hongshan culture. Among the Neolithic jades, the different alien species and the integration of different kinds of biological modeling were relatively rare, but in the late Neolithic period, extraterrestrial spacecraft modeling occurred. This development gives us very important information. Hongshan cultural jade pig-dragon, C-shaped dragon and Y-shaped pendant are actually the integration of different types of biological modeling; they belong to the scope of Pan-Hongshan cultural jade works. This kind of jade also occurred in other archaeological cultures. Particularly the Animal Mask in Liangzhu culture was an alien image. It was the main totem in the original religion of Liangzhu cultural district, and its image can be found on almost all kind of jade works in Liangzhu cultural district. It was also the man's totem, and the symbol of the sun. The animal mask often combined with bird totems to show it came from outer space. In particular Figure 2.35 of Volume Ⅱ is a combinative totem of bird and animal, which was decorated on a Bi with the shape of UFO, and it added some more mysteries to Liangzhu culture. Look closely, we can see that the eyes of the animal mask and the eyes of the Hongshan cultural pig-dragon are nearly the same. Both of them are the inheritance of Pan-Hongshan culture. The jade pig-dragon was not only a clan totem and an amulet but also a symbol of the male. When Liangzhu ancestors had entered the patriarchal society, they chose the pig-dragon's shape as the main part of their totem, in order to achieve peace and prosperity.

During the middle Liangzhu cultural period, its social organization had transited from the coalition of clan to the relative concentration of power in a royal regime. The totem sign had also been correspondingly changed, on the top of the animal mask a majestic king was added, and its profile looks like a Chinese writing "King" character, and its shape looks like a flying bird, which means that he is a messenger from outer space. The kingship was deified. Some pieces of Shandong Longshan cultural jade also had the similar totem images; they had the same morals, i.e. to integrate the clan totem, male totem and deified king into one.

In the middle and late Neolithic period, a special form of Bi occurred, which can be called "convex inner edge disc". It looks like two circular plates face to face together. This kind of Bi had been lasted until the Shang Dynasty; many of them were unearthed from Sanxingdui site. In fact, the shape of the convex inner edge disc is a kind of alien spacecraft (UFO). Moreover, some kinds of Bi whose edges were chamfered have the same meaning. In this book, we also chose a convex inner edge disc of Longshan culture in square round shape (Volume Ⅲ Figure 3.47), and two pieces of Bi whose outer edge was decorated with some winged angels (Volume Ⅲ Figures 3.45, 3.46). Clearly, the Bi stands for an alien spacecraft. These models have some realistic elements. The modeling of winged angel also began in the Pan-Hongshan cultural period. Among the Pan-Hongshan cultural jade works, the modeling of winged angel was not uncommon (Volume Ⅰ Figure 1.33). The inheritance of this art form lasted a long time, such as the modeling of winged angels of the Han Dynasty, and the Flying Angels, Wonderful Sound Birds in Buddhist art and so on.

In short, the Neolithic period is a very important period in human history. During this period, our ancestors inherited the past human civilization and opened up a new round of human civilization. Pan-Hongshan culture is the source of Chinese civilization and it is also the source of Chinese jade culture. Although it was destroyed in the disaster at the end of Last Glacial, and transferred only part of the factors of its civilization to the Neolithic period, the partial cultural heritage was decisive for all human existence and development. Chinese jade culture is a unique Chinese culture, and for the time of the absence of writing records of the prehistoric period, its importance was particularly highlighted. Especially in the middle and late Neolithic period, Chinese jade culture had been prosperous in many areas of China. A lot of Neolithic jade works provided much cultural information for us. If we could correctly interpret this information, we would get a fairly complete vivid image of the Neolithic Chinese civilization history. The title of this series is *The series of Neolithic Jade Records of China*, which means that Chinese ancestors made the historic records of creating Neolithic civilization by means of jade objects.

A　人物造像与氏族图腾

这部分玉器以山东龙山文化与湖北龙山文化(石家河文化)为主,其中人物造像多是东夷太昊氏、少昊氏与凿齿氏形象。太昊族以龙、虎、鸟为图腾,少昊族是太昊族的沿袭,少昊氏族多以鸟类为图腾,凿齿氏以野猪为图腾,他们与豕韦氏是同一氏族集团。从石家河的凿齿氏造型看,他们以虎为图腾,即是说凿齿氏的一个分支以虎为图腾。新石器时期早期,西北地区的古羌族有一部分迁往山东,他们以牛、羊为氏族图腾,他们也融入了东夷集团。以上的动物图腾形象在这一部分均可见到,特别是人首龙身的伏羲造像首次出现在龙山文化玉器中。

东夷族有悠久的制玉传统,他们在泛红山文化时期就有发达的制玉工艺,新石器时期很多人物造像沿袭了泛红山文化玉器的造型与工艺,如图3.7与图3.16以及凿齿氏的头像都明显地继承了泛红山文化玉器的造型与风格。图3.1是一套山东龙山文化玉钺组,其上饰有人物、动物图腾和文字。它为我们提供了有关山东地区氏族成员的重要信息,也使我们了解到石家河文化与山东龙山文化的同源性,所以石家河文化玉器也表现出较高的制玉水平。为了表明氏族的延续,这里也选用了几件商周时期的作品。

新石器时期龙山文化区也十分重视人口的增殖,生殖崇拜与性崇拜的玉器也是常与图腾崇拜的造型整合在一起的。如鸟是氏族图腾,它也代表男性;又如虎、牛均为氏族图腾,但虎头又表示男性生殖器的龟头,牛角又表示雄风等。

A　Figure Statues and Clan Totems

The majority of jade pieces in this Volume are Shandong Longshan cultural jade and Hubei Longshan cultural jade. Most figures belong to Dongyi nationality, such as Taihao's, Shaohao's, and Zaochi's and so on. The Taihao's totems are dragon, tiger, and birds. Shaohao's was Taihao's descendant; most clans of Shaohao took birds for their totems. Zaochi's was with the boar as their totem, and Shiwei's belong to the same clan. A branch of the Zaochi's lived in Shijiahe cultural area, their totem is tiger. In the early Neolithic period, a part of ancient Qiang people living in Northwest of China moved to Shandong area, whose totems were cattle and sheep, and they integrated into the Dongyi family. These totems mentioned above can be seen in this Volume. In particular the Fu xi image with the human head and dragon body first appeared among the Longshan cultural jade.

The Dongyi nationality had a long tradition of the jade-making; they had developed jade craft since the Pan-Hongshan culture period. During the Neolithic period, many human images and technologies were based on Pan-Hongshan jade culture, such as Figures 3.7, 3.16 have obvious succession. Figure 3.1 is a set of jade axe group of Shandong Longshan culture decorated with figures, totems and writings; it provided us with important information, such as the composition of the clans in Shandong area, also showing that the Hubei Shijiahe culture and the Shandong Longshan culture were homology, so Shijiahe jade culture also showed a high level. In order to show the continuation of the clans, a few of jade works in Shang and Zhou Dynasties were selected in this section.

The proliferation of the population was still a highly regarded event in Longshan cultural district during the Neolithic period. The reproduction worship and sex worship were often together with the totem worship. E.g. the bird is clan's totem, and it also represents the male; the tiger and ox are the clan's totems, but the tiger head also represents the male genital, and the ox horn represents the male masculinity.

3.1 玉钺组（山东龙山文化）（图3.1）

这组玉钺共六件，外形相同，尺寸近似。高6~6.3 cm，刃宽4.2~4.4 cm，厚0.2~0.4 cm。黄玉，全沁呈浅棕色，有灰皮。

钺之刃部呈弧形，肩部两端呈圆角，上端均有一对钻孔。钺一、二饰浮雕鹰，两面纹饰相同，是典型的少昊氏鸷鸟图腾像。钺一所饰之鹰形与现藏美国佛利尔美术馆的一件圭上所饰之鹰形同。钺三饰高冠东夷领袖像，可能是少昊像，该钺两面纹饰相同。钺四正面饰牛首；钺五正面饰牛角虎齿饕餮；钺六正面饰牛角虎齿人像。钺四、五、六的反面均饰阴刻"虘""敄"两字（音：巨、潘）。钺一、二、三明确表示出这组玉钺属山东龙山文化少昊集团玉器。因为这六件玉钺为一组，故知牛氏族与虎氏族也是少昊族 的支系。从钺四、五、六来看，"虘""敄"两字是与虎、牛相关的徽铭文字。"虘"字上部是虎字头，下部是"且"字，甲骨文中"且"即"祖"，故"虘"字是以虎为图腾祖先的氏族。"敄"字据专家考证，它是东夷的一支"方夷"的徽铭文字。方夷是发明平板舟的氏族，"敄"字上端的"北"表示平板舟，该氏族以其发明为族徽。"敄"字似与牛无关，笔者认为"敄"族可能是渔业与农业两者兼有的氏族，牛也是其氏族图腾之一。"虘、敄"两字同时出现是因为他们有联姻关系。值得注意的是，在商周

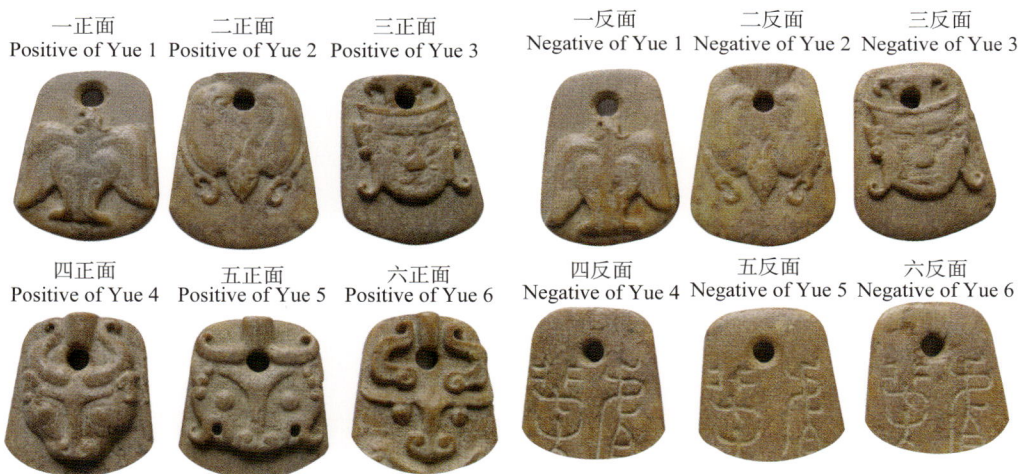

| 一正面 Positive of Yue 1 | 二正面 Positive of Yue 2 | 三正面 Positive of Yue 3 | 一反面 Negative of Yue 1 | 二反面 Negative of Yue 2 | 三反面 Negative of Yue 3 |
| 四正面 Positive of Yue 4 | 五正面 Positive of Yue 5 | 六正面 Positive of Yue 6 | 四反面 Negative of Yue 4 | 五反面 Negative of Yue 5 | 六反面 Negative of Yue 6 |

图 3.1　玉钺组

Figure 3.1　A group of Yue（Shandong Longshan culture）

时期,金文中的氏族徽铭文字在龙山文化时期已经出现。

这组玉钺对于我们了解龙山文化时期的氏族关系十分重要。它使我们了解到以鹰、虎、牛等为图腾的氏族同属少昊集团,凿齿氏也属少昊集团。龙山文化时期他们分布很广,主要在东部沿海地区、长江中下游地区及巴蜀地区,包括山东、湖北龙山文化区,良渚文化区,江淮文化区与巴蜀文化区等地。在这些文化区我们都可见到有关这些图腾的玉器造型。

3.1 A Group of Yue (Shandong Longshan Culture)（Figure 3.1）

There are six pieces of Yue in the group; they have the same shape and similar size.

Height: 6—6.3 cm, blade width: 4.2—4.4 cm, thickness: 0.2—0.4 cm.

They are made of topaz with corrosive light brown and gray skin.

The shape of these pieces of Yue is convex curved blade, rounded corners of shoulder, and a bifacial hole on the middle near the shoulder.

Yue 1 and 2 were decorated with relief typical Shaohao clan's eagle images, and both sides with the same images. The shape of the eagle on Yue 1 is the same as the shape of eagle decorated on a jade Gui in the Freer Art Gallery, U.S.. Yue 3 was decorated a relief Dongyi leader portrait which wore a high crown, may be Shaohao's image, and both sides with the same images. Yue 4 was decorated with an ox head; Yue 5 was decorated with a tiger head with a pair of buffalo horns; Yue 6 was decorated with a human face with tiger fangs and ox horns. The other sides of Yue 4, 5 and 6 were decorated with incised "Ju, Pan" two old Chinese characters, which are the clan's names. Yue 1, 2 and 3 clearly showed that the group of jade Yue belongs to Shandong Longshan cultural district of Shaohao family and we can know that the clans with the tiger or ox as their totem were the branches of Shaohao family. The character "Ju" means that the tiger is their clan's totem; and the character "Pan" means that the "Pan" clan was the inventor of the ship which is made of wood boards. The "Ju" and "Pan" were often put together to show that they are united clan. It is noteworthy that the inscriptions incised on the bronze devices in the Shang and Zhou Dynasties had emerged in Longshan culture period.

This group of jade Yue is very important for understanding the clan relations. It makes us understand that the clans with the tiger or eagle or ox as their totem belong to Shaohao family, and the Zaochi Clan also belongs to Shaohao family. During the Longshan culture period, they were widely distributed, mainly in the eastern coast areas, the middle and lower reaches of Yangtze River and Sichuan region, including Shandong and Hubei Longshan cultural areas, Liangzhu cultural area, Jianghuai cultural area and Bashu cultural area and so on. The jade pieces related to these totemic shapes have been discovered in these areas.

3.2　凿齿氏面具形带饰（山东龙山文化）（图 3.2）

高 5.2 cm，宽 4.6 cm，厚 2.1 cm。

青玉，棕、灰沁色，有灰皮。

造型为一头生羊角的圆雕凿齿氏头像，背面为一凹槽，其上方有一自头顶至下颏的扁方棱，可穿在腰带上。面部纹饰以减地、浮雕、镂空、打洼及阴刻等方法饰出，其形为双目圆凸，鼻梁下凹，鼻孔外翻，双眉覆盖前额，呈火焰形。张大口，唇上方隆起，其上饰点状毛孔纹，门齿两侧有一对獠牙外呲，舌尖上卷，两腮有上扬的云纹胡须，双耳自太阳穴斜插至额头两侧。头顶有一对卷曲的羊角，其上饰竹节纹及点纹。双耳旁有一对佩饰孔。

此图腾造像是炎帝羌族与凿齿氏联合氏族图腾。炎帝是农业氏族，以牛、羊为图腾。炎帝又称烈山氏，因为每年秋收后放火烧掉干枯的禾草以维持土地的肥沃，故火焰也是炎帝的氏族图腾。此玉饰造型奇特，工艺极精湛。

图 3.2　凿齿氏面具形带饰（山东龙山文化）

Figure 3.2　Belt ornament decorated with Zaochi's mask motifs

(Shandong longshan culture)

3.2 Belt Ornament Decorated with Zaochi's Mask Motifs (Shandong Longshan Culture) (Figure 3.2)

Height: 5.2 cm, width: 4.6 cm, thickness: 2.1 cm.

It is made of sapphire with brownish gray markings.

Its shape is a mask of Zaochi's head image with a hollow on its back, and a longitudinal flat ridge on the top of the hollow for wearing. The motifs were decorated with reduce, relief, hollow, embossing, incising, etc. techniques. The shape of the mask is convex round eyes, concave nose bridge, turning out nostrils, flame-shaped eyebrows covering its forehead, opened mouth with a pair of sharp fangs, short beards around its mouth, moiré beards on cheeks, turning up tongue, erect ears with a pair of ear holes, and a pair of curly ram horns on the head which were decorated with bamboo and dots patterns.

This image is joint clan totemic image of the Qiang Clan of Emperor Yan family and Zaochi Clan; Emperor Yan was the agricultural clan with ox and sheep as their totem, and also known as Lieshan, which means to burn the dry grasses after harvest each year to maintain the fertility of the land, so the flame was also the Emperor Yan Clan's totem. This ornament has peculiar shape and very exquisite craftsmanship.

3.3　凿齿氏头像（石家河文化）（图 3.3）

高 5 cm，宽 3.6 cm，厚 2.6 cm。

青白玉，棕、红沁色。

造型为一圆雕凿齿氏头像。其形为双目圆凸，蒜头鼻，鼻孔外翻，咧嘴露齿，上齿有一对獠牙，下颌有须，须分两岔，须端上勾。头顶有一椭圆形发髻，两缕长发披于面颊两侧，末端弯向脑后，前额与脑后均有刘海，脑后还有一对弯钩状发型。自头顶中央至下颌中央有一对钻直孔。比较此造型与图 3.19 虎头的造型可以看出，二者的鼻、口、齿形同，故知凿齿氏的这一个分支以虎为图腾。

图 3.3　凿齿氏头像（石家河文化）

Figure 3.3　Zaochi's portrait (Shijiahe culture)

3.3　Zaochi's Portrait (Shijiahe Culture)（Figure 3.3）

Height: 5 cm, width: 3.6 cm, thickness: 2.6 cm.

It is made of light green jade with corrosive reddish brown markings.

It is a Zaochi's head image, whose shape is convex round eyes, garlic-shaped nose with turning out nostrils, grinning teeth, upper teeth with a pair of fangs, bifurcated hook-shaped beard on the chin, oval-shaped bun on the top, two wisps of hair hanging on both sides of cheeks and bending to the back of head, forehead and back of head with bands, and a pair of curved hook-shaped hairstyle on the back of head. There is a vertical straight central drilling hole from the top to the bottom. Comparing with the tiger head showed in Figure 3.19, it can be seen that they have the same shape of nose, mouth and teeth, so we know that a branch of Zaochi Clan was with the tiger as its totem.

3.4 凿齿氏面具形带饰(石家河文化)(图 3.4)

高 7 cm,宽 6.5 cm,厚 0.3~0.7 cm。

青白玉,棕色沁色,有灰皮。

造型为一片状凿齿氏面像。正面弧凸,反面内凹。反面中央凸起一长方形棱,其上镂空一扁孔,可穿在腰带上。面部纹饰以减地、剔地、打洼、阴刻等技法饰出。以剔地法饰出一双大目,眼角呈钩状,睛珠圆凸。鼻梁顶端呈尖状,鼻孔外翻,"八"字胡,张口露齿,上齿有一对獠牙。头顶有一对卷曲的羊角,其上饰纽丝纹,额头中间有一凸块,呈倒梯形,其上饰瓦沟纹。此图腾面像与图 3.2 的图腾面像有相同的寓意。

3.4 Belt Ornament Decorated with Zaochi's Mask Motifs (Shijiahe Culture) (Figure 3.4)

Height: 7 cm, width: 6.5 cm, thickness: 0.3—0.7 cm.

It is made of light green jade with corrosive brown and gray markings.

It is a plaque of Zaochi's facial image. Its surface is convex, and its back is concave. On the center of back, there is a vertical protruding rectangular ridge on which there is a hollow flat slot for wearing on the belt. The shape of the face is round protruding eyes, high nose bridge, turned out nostrils; curly moustache, opened mouth with protrusive tongue, grinning teeth and a pair of fangs, a pair of curly ram horns with spiral patterns on the top of the head, and an inverted trapezoidal bump decorated with corrugations on the middle of the forehead. The motifs were decorated with relief, reducing, embossing and incising, etc. techniques. This totemic facial mask has the same moral as the mask showed in Figure 3.2.

图 3.4 凿齿氏面具形带饰(石家河文化)

Figure 3.4 Belt ornament decorated with Zaochi's mask motifs (Shijiahe culture)

3.5 戴羽冠人头像（石家河文化）（图 3.5）

高 3.1 cm，宽 3 cm，最厚 1.8 cm。

青玉，全沁呈棕色，有蚀斑、蚀纹。

造型为一头戴"凸"字形羽冠的人头像，其横断面呈钝角等腰三角形。正面人像形为蒜头鼻，鼻梁高凸，水滴状双目，宽眉，弯月形嘴，嘴角上翘，露齿，双耳饰一对耳环。帽顶饰云纹，其两侧饰回纹及下垂的飘带，纹饰以阴刻法饰出。颈部呈圆台形。自头顶中央至颈部中央有一直孔。反面平光。此头像与湖北天门石家河出土的一件头像形似，故知其为石家河文化玉器。美国佛利尔美术馆也有一件头像与此形同。

3.5 Human Head Pendant (Shijiahe Culture) (Figure 3.5)

Height: 3.1 cm, width: 3 cm, maximum thickness: 1.8 cm.

It is made of sapphire with corrosive brown skin and spots.

The shape of the modeling is a human head pendant with a high convex crown on the top; its cross-section is an obtuse isosceles triangle. Its shape of the facial is drop-shaped eyes, wide eyebrows, garlic-shaped nose, high nose bridge, crescent-shaped concave mouth and grinning teeth, and wearing a pair of earrings. The crown was decorated with moire patterns, and sagging streamer patterns were decorated on cheeks. The neck is in round mesa shape, and its back side of the pendant is plain. There is a vertical straight drilling hole from the center of the top to the bottom. This pendant is similar to that one which was unearthed from Shijiahe site, so we know that it is Shijiahe culture jade. The other one with the same shape as this one is in Freer Art Gallery, U.S..

图 3.5 戴羽冠人头像（石家河文化）

Figure 3.5 Human head pendant (Shijiahe culture)

3.6　戴牛角冠人面像（石家河文化）（图 3.6）

高 4.4 cm，宽 4 cm，厚 2.5 cm。

白玉，棕、红沁色，俗称牛毛血丝纹。

造型为一头戴牛角冠的人面像佩饰。其横断面呈折角形，背面为一凹槽，颈部呈半圆弧形。正面人像形为双目圆凸，高眉骨，双眉相接，眉梢上弯，眉上饰细线波纹。高鼻梁，蒜头鼻，颧骨隆起，下颏前翘，"八"字形嘴，嘴角呈云纹形上弯，鼻与上唇之间有一沟槽。一双大耳贴于面颊两侧，头戴饰牛角的"W"形冠，冠之正面中央有一漏斗孔。此人面玉饰的表现方法与工艺特点属石家河文化玉作。

3.6　Mask with an Ox-horn Cap Decoration（Shijiahe Culture）（Figure 3.6）

Height: 4.4 cm, width: 4 cm, thickness: 2.5 cm.

It is made of white jade with corrosive reddish brown markings, commonly known as bloodshot markings.

This modeling is a man face mask which was decorated an ox-horn cap, and the back surface is concave. Its cross-section is in angular shape, and the neck is in semicircular shape. The shape of the facial is round convex eyes, connected high eyebrows decorated with corrugated patterns; high nose bridge, garlic-shaped nose, bulged cheeks, and chin bending forward, W-shaped mouth, a short groove between the mouth and nose, big ears affixed to the cheeks. The cap is decorated with a pair of ox horns and a funnel-shaped drilling hole on the middle. The shape and techniques of this pendant have the characteristics of Shijiahe cultural jade works.

图 3.6　戴牛角冠人面像（石家河文化）

Figure 3.6　Mask with an ox-horn cap decoration (Shijiahe culture)

3.7 戴双鹰首折角冠女子头像（石家河文化）（图3.7）

高 4.3 cm，宽 3 cm，厚 1.1 cm。

黑绿玉，棕、红沁色。

造型为一女子圆雕头像，该女子眉目清秀，吊梢眼，直鼻，弯月形口，口角上翘，笑逐颜开，双耳饰一对耳环。颈部较长，头戴双鹰首折角冠。自头顶至颈下中央有一直孔。双鹰首折角冠是东夷少昊族的标志。此雕像形象生动、可爱，属龙山文化玉作之精品。此造像源于泛红山文化时期（《红山文化玉记》图 1.10）。湖北荆州博物馆有一件与此相同的人面玉饰。

3.7 Woman Head Portrait (Shijiahe Culture) (Figure 3.7)

Height: 4.3 cm, width: 3 cm, thickness: 1.1 cm.

It is made of greenish black jade with corrosive brownish red markings.

It is a three-dimensional woman head portrait. She has a beautiful happy face, whose shape is sloping up eyes, straight nose, upturned crescent-shaped mouth, long neck, wearing a pair of earrings and a double eagle head-shaped crown. There is a drilling hole from top of head to the centre of bottom. The double eagle head-shaped crown was the symbol of Shaohao Clan. This portrait is very lively and lovely; it is the fine jade work of Longshan culture. This kind of human portrait originated from the Pan-Hongshan cultural period (Figure 1.10 in *The Hongshan Cultural Jade Record*). There is a piece of jade woman head portrait in Jingzhou Museum, Hubei Province, which is the same as this one.

图 3.7　戴双鹰首折角冠女子头像
（石家河文化）

Figure 3.7　Woman head portrait
(Shijiahe culture)

图 3.8　戴月牙冠人头像（石家河文化）

Figure 3.8　Woman head portrait

(Shijiahe culture)

3.8　戴月牙冠人头像（石家河文化）（图 3.8）

高 5 cm，宽 3.5 cm，厚 1.8 cm。

青玉，棕色沁色，有灰皮。

造型为一女子面像，其背面有一管状玉珠，这种造型始于泛红山文化时期。该面像眉目清秀，一双吊梢眼，睛珠高凸，直鼻，小口，云纹双耳饰有一对耳环。头戴月牙冠，其上饰纵向阳纹。背面玉珠有一对钻直孔。该造像采用了多种工艺技法，如圆雕、减地、压地、打洼、阴刻等，且磨光度高，是石家河玉作之精品。石家河六合遗址曾出土一件戴月牙冠人面像，其造型和工艺与此件相同。

3.8　Woman Head Portrait（Shijiahe Culture）（Figure 3.8）

Height: 5 cm, width: 3.5 cm, thickness: 1.8 cm.

It is made of sapphire with corrosive brown and gray markings.

This modeling is a woman facial image with a tubular bead on the back, and this kind of modeling originated from the Pan-Hongshan cultural period. It is a beautiful woman face, whose shape is sloping up eyes, straight nose, small mouth, moiré-shaped ears with a pair of earrings, and wearing a crescent-shaped crown with relief feather patterns on it. There is a straight drilling hole on the back of bead. The motifs were decorated by a variety of craft techniques, such as hollow, reducing, embossing, incising, etc. and well burnished. A human facial image ornament was unearthed from Shijiahe Liuhe site; it has the same shape and techniques with this one.

3.9 戴羽冠双面人像（石家河文化）（图 3.9）

高 6.7 cm，最宽 7.5 cm，厚 1.8 cm。

青玉，棕、灰沁色，有灰皮、蚀斑及蚀孔。

造型为一片状双面雕人像，两面纹饰相同。其形为卵形双目，眼角下勾，睛珠呈环状。鼻呈三角形，扁方形口，微张露齿，下颏前翘，面颊隆起。双耳呈三角形，其上饰尖折纹，戴一对大耳环。头戴"介"字形羽冠，其上饰纵向阴纹。羽冠以剔地、浮雕饰出。额头有一"X"形符号，有信仰太阳神的寓意。此造像属石家河文化玉作，它明显地受到良渚文化的影响，如眼形、羽冠均具有良渚文化玉器风格。

图 3.9 戴羽冠双面人像（石家河文化）

Figure 3.9 Double-side portrait (Shijiahe culture)

3.9 Double-side Portrait（Shijiahe Culture）（Figure 3.9）

Height: 6.7 cm, maximum width: 7.5 cm, thickness: 1.8 cm.

It is made of sapphire with corrosive brownish gray markings and gray spots.

It is a double-side carved portrait with the same images on both sides. Its shape is drop-shaped eyes, ring-shaped eye beads, triangle-shaped nose, flat rectangular mouth and grinning teeth, chin bending forward, bulged cheeks, fold angular-shaped ears with a pair of big earrings, wearing an eagle-shaped crest with short vertical feather patterns, and an X symbol on its forehead, which means the worship of sun god. This ornament belongs to Shijiahe cultural jade; it is clearly influenced by the Liangzhu cultural jade, for example, its eyes and crest are in Liangzhu jade style.

图 3.10 饰人像匕首（山东龙山文化）

Figure 3.10 Dagger decorated with portrait (Shandong Longshan culture)

3.10 饰人像匕首(山东龙山文化)(图 3.10)

长 9.5 cm，末端宽 2.2 cm，最厚 0.8 cm。

白玉，质优，棕、黑沁色。

此匕首中间厚边缘薄，锋部倒角呈尖状，末端中央有一凸榫，其上有一横向对钻孔。接近末端的两面均饰一东夷领袖面像，其形为长脸，圆目，蒜头鼻，口微张，下颔前翘，耳呈波纹形，长发披于脑后，发端上勾，头戴平顶帽。此人像与美国佛利尔美术馆馆藏的一件龙山文化玉刀上的人像相同。

3.10 Dagger Decorated with Portrait (Shandong Longshan Culture)(Figure 3.10)

Length 9.5 cm, shoulder width: 2.2 cm, maximum thickness: 0.8 cm.

It is made of white jade with corrosive brown and black markings.

The surface of the dagger is convex; the front part was chamfered into acuminate shape, and there is a protruding tenon with a lateral drilling hole on the middle of its shoulder. A Dongyi leader portrait were decorated on both sides near the shoulder, whose shape is long face, round eyes, garlic-shaped nose, mouth slightly open, chin bending forward, corrugated ears, curved long hair hanging on the back of head, and wearing a flat cap. The image is the same as that image decorated on a Longshan cultural jade knife in Freer Art Gallery.

3.11　戴平顶帽蹲姿人（商）（图 3.11）

高 6 cm，宽 1.9 cm，厚 2.5 cm。

青玉，棕、黄沁色，有灰皮。

造型为一戴平顶帽、披发、半蹲男子。其形为吊梢眼，直鼻，闭口，"八"字胡须，方折"回"形耳，头发披于脑后，发端上翘。挺胸，双手叉腰。围绕膝部饰一道弦纹，表示他身穿短裙。头顶有一对钻斜孔。

此玉人的头部造型与图 3.10 匕首上所示人面像形似，但其面部纹饰属商代风格。这表明商代沿袭了龙山文化时期相同的氏族文化。该玉人与法国赛努西博物馆收藏的一件龙山文化玉人形同。

3.11　Squatting Man Wearing a Flat Cap (Shang Dynasty)（Figure 3.11）

Height: 6 cm, width: 1.9 cm, thickness: 2.5 cm.

It is made of sapphire with corrosive brownish yellow markings and gray spots.

This modeling is a man in squatting posture, whose shape is sloping up eyes, straight nose, closed mouth, curly moustache, fret-shaped ears, long hair hanging on the back of head, straightened chest, hands on his waist. An incised ripple pattern is around his knees to stand for the edge of his skirt. There is a slant drilling hole on the top of his head.

The shape of this man's head is similar to the head shape showed in Figure 3.10, which indicates that the Shang Dynasty still followed the clan's culture of the Longshan cultural period. This human statue is the same as the jade statue collected in the Musee Cernuschi, France.

图 3.11　戴平顶帽蹲姿人（商）

Figure 3.11　Squatting man wearing a flat cap (Shang dynasty)

3.12 戴高羽冠双面凿齿氏面像（商）（图 3.12）

高 6.2 cm，最宽 4.1 cm，最厚 0.9 cm。

黄玉，棕色沁色，有灰皮、蚀斑。

造型为一戴高羽冠凿齿氏双面雕人面像，两面纹饰相同，均呈凸弧面。面形为"臣"字目，横眉，眉梢上翘，蒜头鼻，鼻梁细直，口微张露齿，两侧各有一对獠牙。面颊左右有鸟形纹饰，双耳戴耳环。头上羽冠顶端呈凸弧形，其两角内勾，羽冠上饰瓦沟纹。颈下端为一橄榄形台基，使人像可平稳立放。此人像制作采用了镂空、打洼、浮雕、阴刻等多种技法，工艺高超。

此玉饰与 1989 年江西新干大洋洲出土的一件凿齿氏面像形似，属商代作品。另一件收藏于美国史密森宁研究院，与此件形象一致。

3.12 Double-side Zaochi's Portrait（Shang Dynasty）（Figure 3.12）

Height: 6.2 cm, maximum width: 4.1 cm, maximum thickness: 0.9 cm.

It is made of topaz with brown markings and gray spots.

The modeling is a double-side Zaochi's facial portrait with a high crested crown and the same image on both sides, and the surface is convex. Its facial shape is date kernel-shaped eyes with round convex eye beads, sloping up eyebrows, garlic-shaped nose, relief straight nose bridge, mouth slightly open and grinning, and a pair of tusks on each side. Hollow bird-shaped patterns were decorated on both sides of cheeks. He wore a pair of earrings and a high feathered crown decorated with corrugation patterns. There is an olive-shaped pedestal under the neck for standing stably. The portrait was made by various techniques, such as hollow, relief, embossing, incising and so on, and it has the superb craftsmanship.

This jade portrait is similar to that jade portrait which was unearthed from Dayangzhou site, Xingan County, Jiangxi Province in 1989, which was the work of the Shang Dynasty. Another similar one was collected in Smithsonian Institution, Washington.

图 3.12 戴高羽冠双面凿齿氏面像（商）

Figure 3.12 Double-side Zaochi's portrait (Shang dynasty)

3.13　戴鹰形冠人面像（商）（图 3.13）

高 4.1 cm，最宽 4.7 cm，最厚 1 cm。

青玉，全沁呈棕红色，有灰皮。

造型为一戴羽冠人面像，单面雕，背面平光。羽冠呈展翅鹰形，其下方向两侧延伸。人面形为"臣"字目，云纹鼻，张口呲牙，耳之外缘呈波纹状，饰耳环。面部高凸，纹饰采用双勾技法饰出。帽檐下方有一对水滴状孔。羽冠顶端有一对隧孔。此玉饰是商代作品，但仍有龙山文化特色。

图 3.13　戴鹰形冠人面像（商）

Figure 3.13　Human portrait (Shang dynasty)

3.13　Human Portrait (Shang Dynasty)（Figure 3.13）

Height: 4.1 cm, maximum width: 4.7 cm, maximum thickness: 1 cm.

It is made of sapphire with corrosive brownish red markings and gray spots.

This modeling is a human portrait, and its back is plain. The man wears a crested crown which is an eagle with spreading wings. His facial shape is date kernel-shaped eyes with round eye beads, moiré nose, open mouth and grinning, ripple-shaped ears decorated with earrings. The face is highly convex, and the motifs adopted double-line carving techniques, which is the commonly used technique of the jade production in the Shang Dynasty. There is a pair of drop-shaped holes below the crown, and a pair of ox nostril-shaped holes on its top. This jade ornament was the work of the Shang Dynasty, but it still had the style of the Longshan cultural jade.

3.14　梯形双面雕人面像（商）（图 3.14）

高 3.8 cm，最宽 6.8 cm，最厚 1 cm。

青玉，棕、红、黄等沁色。

造型为一梯形双面雕人面像坠饰，其横断面呈梭形，中间厚，两边薄。纹饰以减地阳纹及阴刻线饰出。其形为 "臣" 字目，蒜头鼻，口部以四道横线饰出，胡须以上扬云纹饰出，面部两侧饰镂空鸟形纹。头戴云纹平顶冠，冠呈扁倒梯形，顶部有一凹槽，形如低头展翅之飞鸟。颈部上方有一道弦纹。从顶端中央至底面中央有一直孔。此坠饰与英国大不列颠博物馆的一件龙山文化人面像形似，都是商代作品。此面像是东夷领袖面像，商代统治者多是夷族，故沿袭龙山文化造像。注意到良渚文化也有这类梯形冠状玉饰，这表明商代文化的继承性。良渚文化时期，梯形还是男性的表征。

图 3.14　梯形双面雕人面像（商）

3.14　Trapezoidal Double-side Human Portrait (Shang Dynasty)（Figure 3.14）

Figure 3.14　Trapezoidal double-side human portrait (Shang dynasty)

Height: 3.8 cm, maximum width: 6.8 cm, maximum thickness: 1 cm.

It is made of sapphire with corrosive brown, red, yellow, etc. markings.

This modeling is a trapezoidal double-side human portrait pendant; its cross-section is in shuttle form. The motifs are relief. The facial shape is date kernel-shaped eyes with protruding round eye beads, garlic-shaped nose. The mouth are decorated with four horizontal lines, and the moustache is in moire shape. Both sides of the facial profile are decorated with hollow bird-shaped motifs, and a groove on the neck. There is a straight drilling hole from the center of the top to the bottom. This pendant is similar to that jade human portrait pendant in British Museum; both of them are the works of the Shang Dynasty. This portrait is the image of the Dongyi leader, and most of the Shang rulers were Yi people, so they followed the Longshan cultural statues. It is noteworthy that such trapezoidal jade ornaments were also found in Liangzhu cultural sites, and it indicated the cultural inheritance in the Shang Dynasty. During the Liangzhu cultural period, the trapezoidal jade ornaments were the symbol of male.

3.15　梯形凿齿氏面像（西周）（图 3.15）

高 4.7 cm，宽 7.1 cm，厚 0.3 cm。

优质青玉，棕色沁色，有蚀斑。

造型为一单面雕凿齿氏人像，玉饰轮廓呈倒梯形，正面为凸弧面，背面内凹，背面纵向中央有一长方形凸棱，棱上有一扁长孔，可穿在腰带上。正面人像形为水滴状双目，睛珠圆凸，"八"字眉。宽鼻梁，鼻端呈云纹形。张口呲牙，口角有一对月牙形獠牙。耳呈波纹状，双耳戴环。头戴平顶帽，其上饰斜线纹，两侧饰镂空鸟形纹。鼻翼两侧饰云纹，面颊两侧有轮廓纹。纹饰主要采用镂空、浅浮雕、压地、阴刻等技法饰出。整体观之，此玉饰似一面具。西周时期的陕西沣西和沣镐遗址有类似的玉器出土，此器当属西周玉器。

图 3.15　梯形凿齿氏面像（西周）

Figure 3.15　Trapezoidal Zaochi's portrait (Western Zhou dynasty)

3.15　Trapezoidal Zaochi's Portrait (Western Zhou Dynasty)（Figure 3.15）

Height: 4.7 cm, width: 7.1 cm, thickness: 0.3 cm.

It is made of high-quality sapphire with corrosive brown markings and spots.

The modeling is a Zaochi's portrait. Its profile is in inverted trapezoidal shape. The positive side is convex surface, and the back side is concave. On the center of the back, there is a protruding vertical rectangular ridge with a hollow slot on it, which can be used for wearing on belt. The shape of the portrait is drop-shaped eyes with round convex eye beads, sloping down eyebrows, wide nose bridge and moiré nose, opened mouth and grinning teeth, a pair of crescent-shaped tusks on both sides of the mouth, corrugated ears with a pair of earrings, and wearing a flat cap which was decorated with diagonal lines on it; the hollow bird-shaped patterns were decorated on the side edges, and contour lines on the cheek sides. The hollow, bas-relief, embossing, incising, etc. techniques were adopted. Overall it seems like a mask. The similar jade portraits were unearthed from Fengxi and Fenggao sites, Shaanxi Province; they belong to Western Zhou Dynasty's jade works.

3.16 双面雕女子面像（大汶口文化）（图 3.16）

高 4.5 cm，宽 5.5 cm，厚 0.5 cm。

青玉，有黑斑，棕色沁色，有灰皮、蚀斑。

造型为一片状双面雕女子面像，两面纹饰相同，轮廓呈倒梯形。其面形为橄榄形双目，眼角相连，三角形鼻，半圆形口，上唇平直，下唇上弯，口微张，呈微笑状。头发中分贴于面颊两侧，发际中央有一直孔。

此人像与山东滕县大汶口文化遗址出土的一件单面雕人像形同，玉质也相似，故应属大汶口文化玉器。此人像与本丛书图 1.41 和图 1.51 人面像形似，但工艺不同。这证明了大汶口文化玉作的继承性。

图 3.16 双面雕女子面像（大汶口文化）

Figure 3.16 Double-side woman portrait (Dawenkou culture)

3.16 Double-side Woman Portrait（Dawenkou Culture）（Figure 3.16）

Height: 4.5, width: 5.5 cm, thickness: 0.5 cm.

It is made of sapphire with corrosive black and brown markings and gray spots.

This modeling is a double-side carving plaque of woman portrait, which has two sides with the same images and inverted trapezoid profile. Its facial shape is connected olive-shaped eyes, triangle-shaped nose, semicircle-shaped mouth, upper lip straight and lower lip concave, mouth slightly open, showing a smile face; the hair from center hanging to the sides and affixed to the cheeks, and a straight drilling hole on the middle of the hair edge.

This portrait is the same as the portrait plaque in shape and jade which was unearthed from Dawenkou cultural site, Teng County, Shandong Province, so it should be Dawenkou cultural jade. This portrait is similar to the portraits showed in Figures 1.41 and 1.51, but the process is different. It proves the inheritance of Dawenkou jade culture.

3.17　环状人首龙形耳饰（山东龙山文化）（图 3.17）

　　图中两件玉饰的玉质、造型与纹饰皆相同，尺寸略异。右：高 6.5 cm，最宽 4.6 cm，厚 1.2 cm。左：高 6.4 cm，最宽 4.4 cm，厚 1.2 cm。碧玉，棕色沁色，有灰皮。

　　造型为一人首盘龙，头尾相接，龙身的横断面呈椭圆形。人首形为水滴状环形双目，睛珠呈圆形。额头隆起，凹鼻梁，鼻端呈卷云纹形。口角上勾，面颊饰钩状云纹，纹饰以压地与阴刻法饰出。头戴平顶帽，其上以打洼法饰出三道凸弦纹，帽顶端有一穗带，其间有一扁孔。此玉饰与台北故宫的一件龙山文化玉圭上凿齿氏领袖所戴耳饰相同，故知其为耳饰。其寓意应是东夷祖先太昊伏羲图腾像。此玉饰的造型显然受到泛红山文化玉器的影响，它沿袭了泛红山文化玉器中猪龙与伏羲的造型（《红山文化玉记》图 1.40、图 1.30）。

图 3.17　环状人首龙形耳饰（山东龙山文化）

Figure 3.17　Dragon-shaped earrings (Shandong Longshan culture)

3.17　Dragon-shaped Earrings (Shandong Longshan Culture) (Figure 3.17)

The two pieces of earrings are with the same jade, shape and decorations; only a little different in size.

(1) Right one

Height: 6.5 cm, maximum width: 4.6 cm, thickness: 1.2 cm.

(2) Left one

Height: 6.4 cm, maximum width: 4.4 cm, thickness: 1.2 cm.

They are made of dark green jade with corrosive brown markings and gray spots.

This modeling is a dragon with human head and its body curved into ring shape. The cross-section of its body is in oval shape. The shape of the human head is ring-shaped eyes with round eye beads, bulged forehead, concave nose bridge, moiré nose, curved hook-shaped mouth, and wearing a flat cap which was decorated with three corrugations and a braid with a drilling hole on the top. The cheeks were decorated with hook-shaped moiré patterns. The motifs were decorated with embossing, intaglio, etc. techniques.

There is a portrait image decorated on a jade Gui of Longshan culture collected in Taipei Palace Museum; the image is a Zaochi's leader who wears a pair of earrings with the same shape of this pair; so we can know this is a pair of earrings. The moral should be the Taihao's totemic image; Taihao Fuxi was the ancestor of Dongyi family. This ornament was obviously influenced by the Pan-Hongshan cultural jade; it followed the shapes of pig-dragon and Fuxi image of Pan-Hongshan cultural jade (Figures 1.30 and 1.40 in *The Hongshan Cultural Jade Record*).

3.18 玦形独角龙（山东龙山文化）（图 3.18）

高 5.5 cm，宽 5 cm，中心孔径 1.3 cm。

青玉，棕色沁色，有灰皮、蚀斑、蚀孔及冰裂纹。

其造型略似红山文化玉猪龙，呈玦形，但头型与工艺不同。此龙头形为圆目，长鼻，鼻口部饰有五道弦纹，头顶生一角，呈弯钩形，尖端朝前。背部有一对钻孔。中央圆孔内壁平光。此玉龙的制作显然受到红山文化的影响，考虑到图 3.17 中龙的造型，此玉龙应属山东龙山文化玉器。另外，猪龙是男性的图腾，头上长角在龙山文化中表示雄风。

3.18 Jue-shaped One-horned Dragon Pendant (Shandong Longshan Culture) (Figure 3.18)

Height: 5.5 cm, width: 5 cm, center aperture: 1.3 cm.

It is made of sapphire with corrosive brown markings and spots.

Its shape somewhat is similar to the Hongshan cultural jade pig-dragon, but the head shape and process are different. It is in Jue shape. The head shape of the dragon is round eyes, long muzzle decorated with five horizontal incised lines, a hook-shaped horn on the head and pointed forward. There is a bifacial drilling hole on the back. It has been well burnished. The production of the dragon was obviously affected by Hongshan culture. Comparing this pendant with the pendant showed in Figure 3.17, we know it belongs to Longshan cultural jade. In addition, the pig-dragon is the totem of male, and the horn on head implicates the male masculinity.

图 3.18　玦形独角龙（山东龙山文化）

Figure 3.18　Jue-shaped one-horned dragon pendant (Shandong Longshan culture)

3.19 虎头佩(一)(石家河文化)(图 3.19)

高 3.5 cm，宽 4.5 cm，厚 2 cm。

青玉，有黑斑，棕、红沁色。

此虎头为椭球形，似一水子玉随形雕成。虎头形为卵形双目，其上饰有弧线纹和边界纹，睛珠在内侧眼角，呈环形凸起，双目间有凸起的连桥，眼下方有条剔地凸起横贯面颊的波纹，其上饰平行短毛纹。蒜头鼻，短鼻梁，鼻孔外翻。大嘴微张，露齿，嘴角有一对獠牙。额头有两道凸弦纹，双耳贴于头顶两侧，呈卷云纹状。背面浮雕"V"字形纹及波纹。自头顶中央至下额中央有一直孔。此玉虎头造型奇特、威猛，制作多采用剔地和浮雕工艺，工艺难度很大。图 3.3、图 3.4 也有相同的工艺特点。背面的"V"形符号代表男性生殖器，虎头表示雄风。

3.19 Tiger Head Pendant—1 (Shijiahe Culture)(Figure 3.19)

Height: 3.5 cm, width: 4.5 cm, thickness: 2 cm.

It is made of sapphire with corrosive reddish brown markings and black spots.

It is ellipsoid-shaped tiger head pendant; it seems to be a river pebble. The tiger head shape is oval eyes with curved lines on it, convex ring-shaped eye beads on the inside corners of the eyes, a corrugated bump on the glabellum. Below the eyes there is a band of relief ripple, which crossed the cheeks and decorated with short hairs on it, garlic-shaped nose with short nose bridge, turning out nostrils, mouth slightly open and grinningly with a pair of tusks, two relief curved lines on the forehead, curled ears on the top of head. There are two relief V-shaped marks on the back, and a straight drilling hole from the center of the top to the center of the chin. The shape of the tiger head is fierce and strange. The relief, reduction, etc. techniques were used in the production, and the process is very difficult. The pendants showed in Figures 3.3 and 3.4 also have the same technical characteristics. The V-shaped marks decorated on the back means male genitalia, and the tiger head means male masculinity.

图 3.19 虎头佩(一)

（石家河文化）

Figure 3.19 Tiger head pendant—1 (Shijiahe culture)

3.20　虎头佩(二)（石家河文化）（图 3.20）

图中两虎头佩造型、纹饰与工艺皆相同。

左：高 5.4 cm，宽 4 cm，最厚 2 cm。青玉，棕色沁色，有灰皮、蚀斑。

右：高 5.2 cm，宽 3.6 cm，最厚 2 cm。青玉，棕色沁色，有灰皮、蚀斑。

造型为一片状浮雕虎头。虎目高凸，呈水滴状，眼角上挑。直宽鼻，高鼻梁，口是位于鼻下方边棱上的一直孔，直通头顶。额头呈"人"字形高凸，双耳立于额头两侧，饰有凹槽形耳孔。面部周边有一圈阴刻边线纹。背面周边有一圈边界纹，中间有代表男根的双钩纹。此虎头额头上方呈"W"形，似匍匐状弯曲的双腿，眼鼻部似男子勃起的生殖器，整体呈匍匐交媾的形态。

图 3.20　虎头佩(二)（石家河文化）

Figure 3.20　Tiger head pendants—2 (Shijiahe culture)

3.20　Tiger Head Pendants—2（Shijiahe Culture）（Figure 3.20）

The two pieces of tiger head pendants are with the same shape, decoration and process.

（1）Left one

Height: 5.4 cm, width: 4 cm, maximum thickness: 2 cm.

It is made of sapphire with corrosive brown and gray markings and spots.

（2）Right one

Height: 5.2 cm, width: 3.6 cm, maximum thickness: 2 cm.

It is made of sapphire with corrosive brown and gray markings and spots.

The shape is a plaque of tiger head: sloping up convex drop-shaped eyes, straight wide nose with high nose bridge, convex fold angle-shaped eyebrows, long ears standing on both sides of the forehead, and the mouth is a straight drilling hole on the middle of the lower edge and through to the top of head. Around the periphery of the face and back there were decorated with incised boundary lines, and double-hook pattern was decorated on the middle of the back. The upper part of the pendant is in W-shape, like a pair of prostrate bending legs, and the lower part of the pendant is in erected male genitalia shape. The overall shape is in prostrating intercourse posture.

3.21　牛角虎头佩（石家河文化）（图 3.21）

图中的三件佩饰造型、纹饰与工艺皆相同。

佩一：高 4 cm，宽 5.4 cm，厚 1.7 cm。黄玉，橘红沁色，蜡状光泽。

佩二：高 4.4 cm，宽 6.2 cm，厚 1.5 cm。灰绿玉，表面侵蚀较重，有灰皮、蚀斑及蚀孔。

佩三：高 4.5 cm，宽 6.2 cm，厚 1.5 cm。灰绿玉，棕、红沁色，有灰皮。

造型为一片状虎头，轮廓呈扁圆形。虎面形为双目呈袋状凸起，睛珠呈圆形，位于内侧眼角。双眉上扬，其上饰平行短线纹。鼻端呈云纹状，口是位于鼻下方边棱上的一直孔，直通头顶。两侧有胡须。额上有两道波纹，头顶两侧有卷云纹形双耳，额上方有一对牛角。纹饰以压地、剔地、浮雕、阴刻等技法饰出。背面饰双钩纹。造型生动，工艺精湛。

石家河文化玉器虎头的造型很多，他们可能是东夷太昊族的一个分支，以虎为图腾。饰牛角有联合氏族图腾的寓意，同时也有生殖文化的内涵，虎头即为龟头，牛角表示雄风。其背面的双钩纹也是男性生殖器的标示符。此玉虎头以其鼻下方边棱上的一孔表示虎口，其原因就是以此孔暗示尿道口。此类虎头可称为虎头形龟头。美国史密森宁研究院藏一龙山文化片状玉器，其上方是一倒梯形图腾像，下方为长方形，端部为一虎头。其整体造型酷似男性生殖器，龟头部位正是石家河型虎头。我们在总论中讲到，新石器时期的玉器造型常将祖先崇拜、图腾崇拜与生殖崇拜整合在一起。

佩一　　　　　　　　　佩二　　　　　　　　　佩三
Pendant 1　　　　　Pendant 2　　　　　Pendant 3

图 3.21　牛角虎头佩（石家河文化）

Figure 3.21　Tiger head with ox horns pendants (Shijiahe culture)

3.21 Tiger Head with Ox Horns Pendants (Shijiahe Culture) (Figure 3.21)

These three pieces of tiger head pendants are with the same shape, decorations and process.

（1）Pendant 1

Height: 4 cm, width: 5.4 cm, thickness: 1.7 cm.

It is made with topaz with corrosive orange markings and waxy luster.

（2）Pendant 2

Height: 4.4 cm, width: 6.2 cm, thickness: 1.5 cm.

It is made of grayish green jade with corrosive gray skin spots and pits.

（3）Pendant 3

Height: 4.5 cm, width: 6.2 cm, thickness: 1.5 cm.

It is made of grayish green jade with corrosive brownish red markings and gray spots.

The shape is a plaque of tiger head, and the profile is in oval shape. The facial shape is oval convex eyes with round eye beads in the inside corners of the eyes, curved rising eyebrows decorated with short lines and moiré-shaped nose. Mouth is a straight hole on the middle of the lower edge and through to the top, with beards on both sides and two ripple lines on the forehead. Curled-shaped ears are on both sides of the head with a pair of ox horns between the ears. The double-hook pattern is decorated on the back. The relief, embossing, reducing and incising techniques were used in the production. They are in vivid style with high-level technology skills.

There were many tiger head-shaped jade pendants in Shjiahe cultural jade pieces; they may be a branch of Dongyi Taihao family with the tiger as their totem. These pendants decorating tiger head with ox horns have the moral of jointed clan's totem, also have the connotation of reproductive culture. The tiger head means glans, and the ox horns means male masculinity. The double-hook marks also are the symbol of the male genital, and the straight hole-shaped mouth is just like the male urethra. This kind of tiger head could be called tiger head-shaped glans. There is a jade plaque in Smithsonian Institution, Washington. The upper part of the plaque is an inverted trapezoidal totemic image, and the lower part is a rectangular band and decorated with a tiger head on the end of the band. The overall shape is similar to the male genitalia, since the position of the glans exactly is the tiger head, and the shape of the tiger head is in the Shijiahe type. As mentioned in General Remarks, the jade shapes of the Neolithic period were often integrated ancestor worship, totem worship and reproductive worship into one.

3.22　鸟（山东龙山文化）（图 3.22）

高 6 cm，宽 5 cm，厚 2.7 cm。

全沁呈棕、灰色，包浆厚重，原玉质不辨。

鸟之身体浑圆，双翅收于身体两侧，腹部、背部均隆起。鸟首呈球状，双目圆凸，尖喙内勾。双腿呈弧形贴于胸腹部，爪趾呈钩状，以浮雕法饰出。背面以打洼法饰出四道尾羽纹。颈部有一对钻直孔。整体观之，此鸟呈俯冲捉食状。此鸟似一块水子玉随形而作，可谓匠心独具。造型古朴可爱，工艺精良。

图 3.22　鸟（山东龙山文化）

Figure 3.22　Bird pendant (Shandong Longshan culture)

3.22　Bird Pendant（Shandong Longshan Culture）（Figure 3.22）

Height: 6 cm, width: 5 cm, thickness: 2.7 cm.

It is covered by heavy corrosive brownish gray skin; the original jade cannot be seen.

This is a three dimensional bird shape pendant, ellipsoid-shaped body and hemispherical head, wings affixed to the body sides, convex round eyes, pointed beak tip, curved legs affixed to the chest and abdomen, hook-shaped relief claws, and four corrugates patterns are decorated on its tail wing. There is a straight drilling hole on its neck. The overall shape is in diving and catching posture. This modeling has ancient classic beauty, very cute, with exquisite technology.

3.23　鸮（山东龙山文化）（图 3.23）

高 4.7 cm，宽 3.4 cm，厚 0.7 cm。

青白玉，红色沁色，有灰皮。

造型为一片状双面雕立姿鸮，其头呈倒三角形，双目圆凸，双耳立于头顶左右，尖喙。双肩上耸，以打洼法饰出折角形双翅之骨架。双足相对，贴于腹部。尾翼下垂。背面以打洼法饰出双翅、身体与尾翼。双翅饰阴刻折线纹与平行线纹，身体饰横向短线纹。自头顶至尾端有一对钻直孔。此鸮造型生动，工艺精湛。此鸮造型与红山文化玉鸮造型相似，但工艺不同。它们同源自泛红山文化。

图 3.23　鸮（山东龙山文化）

Figure 3.23　Owl pendant (Shandong Longshan culture)

3.23.　Owl Pendant (Shandong Longshan Culture)（Figure 3.23）

Height: 4.7 cm, width: 3.4 cm, thickness: 0.7 cm.

It is made of light green jade with corrosive red markings and gray spots.

This modeling is a double-side carving plaque of standing owl. Its shape is inverted triangle-shaped head, convex round eyes, ears on the sides of the head, sharp beak, shrugging shoulders, fold angle-shaped wings, feet closed together and affixed to the abdomen, and tail wing sagging. There are two vertical grooves on the back which separated the wings and body, and decorated with incised lines on the wings and body. There is a straight drilling hole from the top of head to the end of tail. This owl is in vivid style with high level technology skills. Its shape is similar to the jade owls of Hongshan culture, but in different process. Both of them are originated from Pan-Hongshan culture.

B 礼器

这部分礼器的造型均为立体圆雕玉器,从其表面的厚重包浆及与它们相应的陶器比较可知,它们的制作时间很早。每件作品都造型端庄、美观,且采用难度很大的圆雕、浮雕、镂空等技术,工艺水平极高,又具实用性。另外,动物造型的容器也十分生动可爱。这些玉器的制作水平与同时期其他地区的玉器制作相比,或与相应的陶器制作相比都是远远超过的,可谓鹤立鸡群。读者自然会产生疑问:那时可能有如此高的制玉水平吗?同样的问题也出现在《良渚文化玉记》中的海豚形器中(图2.27)。笔者对此给出的答案是:这些都是泛红山文化的继承。虽然泛红山文化在末次冰期结束时遭到了毁灭,但玉文化仍有部分的继承,这种继承不仅是在红山文化区,在各玉文化发达区均有体现,笔者在总论中已提到了这一点。这里所谓"继承"有两种含义,其一即是尚有泛红山文化玉器留存到新石器时期。书中这部分玉器从玉质看,有些是所谓的熊胆青玉,这是泛红山文化玉器中常见的玉种,所以不能排除这部分玉器中有些是或全部都是泛红山文化玉器的留存。另一种继承是制玉技术的继承,新石器时期尚有部分的巫觋等人掌握了泛红山文化时期的制玉技术,可制作高水平的玉作。如此看来,新石器时期的一些礼仪性的陶器造型很多来自泛红山文化玉器的造型。这更进一步证明了泛红山文化不仅是中华玉文化的源头,而且是中华文明的源头,也即是说,中华文明始自玉文化。笔者所给出的这部分玉器的考古文化类型是相对于相应的陶器类型而言,并不是指该玉器即是当时当地的作品。它们很可能是泛红山文化玉器的遗存。

B Ritual Devices

All of ritual devices in this part are three-dimensional sculptures. From the thick corrosive layer on the jade surface, we know that their production time was very early. The shape of each piece was dignified and beautiful, and adopted the very difficult three-dimensional sculptural craft, such as the relief and open-work techniques; and the process had a very high level. The animal shaped containers were also very lively and cute. Comparing the production level of these jade with other jade-making or corresponding pottery devices in the same period, it was far beyond, and clearly exceeded others. Readers will naturally doubt why they had such a high level of jade-making at that time. The same problem also appeared in the dolphin-shaped device in Volume II *The Liangzhu Cultural Jade Record*（Figure 2.27）. The answer is they were Pan-Hongshan cultural inheritance. There are two implications here for the so-called inheritance. One is that they were the remains of Pan-Hongshan culture. From the jade and process point of view, there is such a possibility. The other is the succession of the process of jade-making. Because some witches or wizards acquired the Pan-Hongshan cultural jade technology and produced the high-level jade during the Neolithic period. From this, we know that many kind of Neolithic pottery style used for ceremonial was from the jade models in Pan-Hongshan culture period. This is the further proof of the fact that Pan-Hongshan culture is not only the source of the Chinese jade culture, but also an important source of Chinese civilization. In other words, Chinese civilization began with jade culture. In this section, the given archaeological culture that the jade pieces belong to, was set by its corresponding Neolithic potteries. We are not sure that they are local works at the same time. These jade pieces maybe are the remains of Pan-Hongshan culture.

3.24　带盖鼎（北辛文化）（图 3.24）

通高 13.2 cm，盖高 6.8 cm。容积 240 mL，盖内容积 180 mL。青玉，全沁呈棕、红色，有灰皮、蚀斑及蚀孔。

鼎身呈直立橄榄球状，鼎体下方有三锥状足。表面饰带状"V"形纹，每条带上饰 4~5 道平行凸起的弦纹，边口内有一道减地台阶，与盖边缘凸起的台阶恰好相合。鼎的内壁呈半球形，磨制光滑。盖上的纹饰与鼎体的纹饰相同，盖顶端有一桥形钮，其上饰 5 组凸弦纹，盖内侧为球面形，边口有一道凸起的台阶。

此玉鼎与北辛文化的一陶鼎形同，故称北辛文化型玉器。这件玉鼎在当时应是一件置于宗庙的重要礼器。北辛文化距今约七千年，那时能制作如此高水平的玉器吗？这似乎是个谜。其谜底即是泛红山文化的传承。

3.24　Tripod with Lid (Beixin Culture)（Figure 3.24）

Height: 13.2 cm, lid height: 6.8 cm, volume: 240 mL, lid volume: 180 mL.

It is made of sapphire with corrosive brownish red markings and spots.

This is a tripod container with an ellipsoid-shaped body and conical-shaped feet; the V-shaped corrugated patterns were decorated on the surface. The edge of the mouth is in concave step shape which just matches the convex step on the lid edge. The inside wall of its body and lid is in hemisphere shape and ground smooth; there is a protruding bridge-shaped button on the top of the lid and decorated with corrugates motifs.

This tripod is the same as the pottery tripod of Beixin culture, so it's called Beixin cultural jade tripod. It was an important ancestral ritual device at that time. Beixin culture was dating back to about seven thousand years ago, why so high level of jade work was there then? This seems to be a mystery; in fact the answer is the inheritance of Pan-Hongshan culture.

图 3.24　带盖鼎（北辛文化）

Figure 3.24　Tripod with lid (Beixin culture)

3.25 带盖长方形盒（大汶口文化）（图3.25）

盒之口缘呈圆角长方形，长 13.4 cm，宽 9.2 cm，高 4 cm，通高 8.5 cm，容积 190 mL。

熊胆青玉，棕、红沁色，有灰皮及漆状亮斑。

盒之外壁呈光滑曲面形，内壁为内凹曲面，磨制光滑。盒之边口有一圈减地台阶，沿外缘口下方有一圈高凸的乳丁纹，共 44 粒乳丁。盒之底面略上凹。上盖圆隆，其边缘有边棱，上方有一圈高凸乳丁纹，共 45 粒乳丁。盖之上下左右四方各有一桥形钮，两大两小，大钮下方为扁孔，小钮下方为圆孔。盖之内缘有一圈减地凸棱，它与盒体之边槽相合。大汶口文化有类似的陶器，故此玉盒为大汶口文化型。

乳丁纹始于马家窑文化陶器，这证明当时善于制陶的陕西羌族一部分曾迁往大汶口文化区。乳丁纹有大地母亲的寓意，它是中华文化中延续最久的纹饰，自仰韶文化时期一直延续到现在。

图 3.25 带盖长方形盒（大汶口文化）

Figure 3.25 Ellipsoidal box with lid (Dawenkou culture)

3.25 Ellipsoidal Box with Lid（Dawenkou culture）（Figure 3.25）

Length: 13.4 cm, width: 9.2 cm, body height: 4 cm, height with lid: 8.5 cm, volume: 190 mL.

It is made of bile-colored jade with corrosive brownish red markings and lacquer-like bright spots.

This is an ellipsoid-shaped jade box. The inside and outside surfaces were ground smooth, and the bottom slightly convex. There is a groove around the rim which just matches the protruding edge on the lid. There are two circles of nipple patterns around the mouth rim on the body and lid respectively. There are four bridge-shaped button distributed in four directions on the lid surface, and two of them are bigger with flat holes, another two smaller with round holes. There are some Dawenkou pottery boxes similar to this one, so it is in Dawenkou cultural type.

The nipple pattern began in Majiayao cultural pottery pattern; it proved that part of Shaanxi Qiang people good for ceramic had moved to Dawenkou cultural district. The nipple pattern has the connotation of the earth and mother, and this pattern has the longest continuation in Chinese culture. It has continued since Yangshao period to the present time.

3.26 带盖罐（大汶口文化）（图 3.26）

高 10.8 cm，罐口为椭圆形，长 12.2 cm，宽 8.2 cm，容积 200 mL。

熊胆青玉，棕、红沁色，有灰皮及漆状亮斑。

罐之外壁呈光滑曲面形，其底面略上凹。罐口有一圈减地台阶，边缘有边棱，其下方有一圈高凸的乳丁纹，共 38 粒乳丁。内壁形似澡盆，磨制光滑。盖口有一圈减地凸棱，用以和罐体密合。沿盖之上边缘有一圈高凸乳丁纹，共 36 粒乳丁。盖顶端有一桥钮，其上饰纽丝绳纹，桥钮下方有一扁孔。盖之两端各有一半圆形小钮，中间有圆孔。此罐造型美观，工艺精致。大汶口文化有类似的陶罐。

3.26 Jar with Lid（Dawenkou Culture）（Figure 3.26）

Height: 10.8 cm, length: 12.2 cm, width: 8.2 cm, volume: 200 mL.

It is made of bile-colored jade with corrosive brownish red markings, and lacquer-like bright spots.

The surface and inside walls of the jar are ground smooth and the bottom slightly concave. There is a step around the mouth rim for matching the convex edge on the lid to seal the rim. There are two circles of nipple patterns around the mouth rim on the body and lid respectively. Inside of the body it looks like a bath-tub. There is a bridge-shaped button with a flat hole on the top of the lid and decorated with spiral patterns, and two small buttons with round holes on the two sides of the lid. This jar has the beautiful shape and exquisite process. The similar pottery jars were found in Dawenkou cultural site.

图 3.26 带盖罐（大汶口文化）

Figure 3.26 Jar with lid (Dawenkou culture)

3.27　鼓腹罐（大汶口文化）（图 3.27）

高 8.1 cm，口径 9.6 cm，底面直径 6 cm，容积 300 mL。

熊胆青玉，棕、红沁色，有灰皮及棕黄色漆状亮斑。

罐形为卷沿，鼓腹。在口缘外侧有一圈高凸的乳丁纹，共有乳丁 29 粒。罐之底面略上凹。内壁呈凹弧面形，磨制光滑。此罐造型规整，工艺精良。它与一大汶口陶罐形似。

图 3.27　鼓腹罐（大汶口文化）

Figure 3.27　Puff Jar（Dawenkou culture）

3.27　Puff Jar（Dawenkou Culture）（Figure 3.27）

Height: 8.1 cm, mouth diameter: 9.6 cm, base diameter: 6 cm, volume: 300 mL.

It is made of bile-colored jade with corrosive brownish red markings and brownish yellow lacquer-like bright spots.

The shape of the jar is out turned mouth rim, bulged abdomen, and decorated with a circle of high convex nipple pattern around the outside of the mouth rim, in a total of 29 nipples; the bottom of the jar is slightly concave; the surface and inside wall were ground smooth. This jar is in neat shape and has exquisite technology. The similar shaped pottery jars were founded in Dawenkou site.

3.28 兽罇（大汶口文化）（图 3.28）

长 15.3 cm，高 11 cm，宽 6.8 cm，重 1200 g，腹内容积 60 mL，口内容积 20 mL。

熊胆青玉，棕、红沁色，有灰皮及漆状亮斑。

外形为一只立姿、仰首、张大口叫的狗。其形为圆头，枣核形镂空双目，短鼻梁，鼻孔外翻。口内镂空一圆槽，与双目连通。内壁为光滑弧面。双耳立于脑后，四肢壮硕，足饰爪趾纹。腹部圆隆，短尾上翘。罇口为直圆管形，立于狗之背部近尾端处，管口外径为 4 cm，内径 3 cm。腹内为一圆槽，槽壁光滑。在狗的颈后与圆管之间有一桥形提梁。此罇造型生动，制作精良，工艺难度高。此罇与大汶口一陶罇形似，故称它是大汶口文化型玉器。

图 3.28 兽罇（大汶口文化）

Figure 3.28 Animal-shaped Zun (Dawenkou culture)

3.28　Animal-shaped Zun (Dawenkou Culture) (Figure 3.28)

Length: 15.3 cm, height: 11 cm, width: 6.8 cm, abdomen volume: 60 mL, mouth volume: 20 mL, weight: 1200 g.

It is made of bile-colored jade with corrosive brownish red markings, gray skin and lacquer-like bright spots.

The shape of the Zun is a standing dog with round head looking up, date kernel-shaped hollow eyes, short nose bridge, turning out nostrils, a hollow groove in the mouth and connected with the eyes, ears erected on the head, sturdy four legs, bulged belly, short tail upturned. The mouth of the Zun is in straight tube shape on the rear of the dog back. The inside of the abdomen is a circular tank, and a bridge-shaped lifting beam on the back. The surface and inside walls are ground smooth. The shape of this Zun is vivid and lovely with high-level techniques. It is similar to a pottery Zun unearthed from Dawenkou site, so it's in Dawenkou cultural type.

3.29　三袋足提梁壶（山东龙山文化）（图 3.29）

长 14.5 cm，最宽 7.2 cm，高 10.5 cm，容积 100 mL。

熊胆青玉，棕、红沁色，有灰皮及漆状亮斑。

外形似一个仰首翘尾的小动物。袋状三足，前二后一，倒看似桃形。壶中间鼓腹，壶颈竖立。壶口前方还有一小口与壶颈相通。两口均呈喇叭口形，在两口外侧饰有一圈高凸的乳丁，共 20 粒。颈部前方呈条状凸起，颈下有一桥形钮，中间有圆孔。壶口上方为直孔，内壁为光滑的弧面。自后袋足上方至壶颈后有一提梁，其上饰纽丝绳纹。此壶外形美观，制作精细，工艺难度很高。

图 3.29　三袋足提梁壶（山东龙山文化）

Figure 3.29　Pot with three bulging legs（Shandong Longshan culture）

3.29　Pot with Three Bulging Legs（Shandong Longshan Culture）（Figure 3.29）

Length: 14.5 cm, maximum width: 7.2 cm, height: 10.5 cm, volume: 100 mL.

It is made of bile-colored jade with corrosive brownish red markings and lacquer-like bright spots.

The shape of the pot looks like a small animal which is looking up and turning up the tail, and has three breast-shaped legs, bulged belly, erected pot neck, a small spout front of the mouth connected with pot neck. Both of the mouth and spout are in funnel shape, with a circle of high convex nipple patterns decorated on the outside around the mouth, and a bridge-shaped button with a round hole on the neck. The upper part in the mouth is a straight hole, whose inner wall is a ground smooth surface, and there is a curved lifting beam on the back and decorated with spiral patterns. This pot has the beautiful appearance, exquisite techniques and very difficult process.

图 3.30　三袋足长颈瓶（山东龙山文化）

Figure 3.30　Flask with three bulging legs (Shandong Longshan culture)

3.30　三袋足长颈瓶（山东龙山文化）（图 3.30）

高 16.2 cm，宽 8.5 cm，9.1 cm。重 1050 g，容积 120 mL。

熊胆青玉，鸡骨白与棕色沁色，有灰皮。

瓶有三袋足，前二后一，足端尖凸。三足上方有一圈凸弦纹，后袋足上方有两道环形凸弦纹。颈口呈直圆管形，颈口上端有高凸的凹面舌形流，管口外缘有边框，以减地法饰出。管口颈部下方有一凸弧面圆槽。颈后有一桥形提梁，其上饰凸起的弦纹。在瓶表面还饰有对称浮雕乳丁纹。此瓶造型美观、规整，工艺精良。此玉瓶与山东龙山文化的一陶瓶形同。

3.30　Flask with Three Bulging Legs（Shandong Longshan Culture）（Figure 3.30）

Height: 16.2 cm, width: 8.5 cm, length: 9.1 cm, weight: 1050 g, volume: 120 mL.

It is made of bile-colored jade with corrosive chicken bone-white, brown and gray skin.

The flask consists of two parts, the upper part and the lower part, the upper part including the neck, mouth and a bridge-shaped handle, the lower part including three bulging legs. Its surface is decorated with bas-relief curve lines and nipple patterns; the handle is in band shape and decorated with corrugated pattern. The surface is ground smooth. The neck is in straight tube shape, a high protruding tongue-shaped nozzle on the front of the mouth, a straight round groove inside the mouth. This flask is in beautiful shape, well-balanced, and has exquisite technology. The shape of this flask is the same as a pottery flask of Shandong Longshan culture.

3.31　饰猿面带盖樽（马家窑文化）（图 3.31）

高 20.8 cm，樽高 16.8 cm，盖高 4.2 cm，口径 6 cm，上端鼓腹宽 8.8 cm，底面直径 4.7 cm，重 1850 g，容积 350 mL。

青玉，棕色沁色，有灰皮、蚀斑。

樽上宽下窄，樽口内敛，形成折肩，鼓腹。在鼓腹外侧均匀凸起四个立柱形凸榫，榫口呈"V"形缺口状，中间有圆槽，应是为装设提梁所用。樽外侧在相对的两面各饰一直立的半椭圆形凹槽，其形似良渚玉珠图 2.97 上的兽面纹。其下方饰一圈凸起的浮雕锯齿纹，共 28 个锯齿。樽底面略内凹。樽内壁磨制光滑。

樽盖呈球冠状，内凹外凸，边缘有凸棱，使之与樽体配合。盖顶端为一片状神人面饰，其形为环状立目，睛珠呈水滴状高凸，双目间有凸起的额头，鼻梁凹陷，鼻孔外翻，口呈"一"字形，微张，其整体形象似一猿面。纹饰皆以浮雕饰出。此樽造型奇特，制作工艺水平高。此器属马家窑文化型。器身所饰的猿面可能是炎帝世系夸父族图腾造像。

图 3.31　饰猿面带盖樽（马家窑文化）

Figure 3.31　Zun with a lid and a totem image decoration（Majiayao culture）

3.31   Zun with a Lid and a Totem Image Decoration (Majiayao Culture) (Figure 3.31)

Height: 20.8 cm, Zun height: 16.8 cm, lid height: 4.2 cm, mouth diameter: 6 cm, upper belly width: 8.8 cm, bottom diameter: 4.7 cm, volume: 350 mL, weight: 1850 g.

It is made of sapphire with corrosive brown markings and spots.

The Zun is in conical shape, and the mouth rim contracted, so formed fold shoulder and bulged belly. There are four convex pole-shaped tenons with V-shaped gap and round hole around the upper belly; they should be used for installation of its lifting beam. Two opposite vertical semi-oval shaped grooves were decorated on the surface, which are similar to the animal mask decoration on the Liangzhu beads showed in Figure 2.97, and a circle of high relief serration pattern was decorated below the grooves. The bottom of the Zun is slightly concave, and the surface and the inner wall are polished smooth.

The lid is in convex coronal shape, with protruding edge for sealing the mouth rim, and a high relief god face is decorated on the top of the lid, whose shape is sloping up drop-shaped eyes with convex eye beads, protruding forehead, turning out nostrils and mouth slightly open. Its overall shape looks like an ape face. The shape of the Zun is peculiar; it has high-level production process. It is Majiayao cultural type jade work. The ape face should be the Kuafu Clan totemic image; the Kuafu Clan was a branch of the Emperor Yan family.

3.32 饰人首带盖樽（马家窑文化）（图 3.32）

高 18 cm，鼓腹宽 9 cm，最宽 13.2 cm，底面直径 5.2 cm，口径 5.5 cm，重 1160 g，容积 280 mL。

青玉，棕、红沁色，有蚀斑、蚀纹。

樽体上粗下细，樽口内敛，形成上端折肩，鼓腹。在鼓腹的一面有一竖向桥钮，钮孔呈扁圆形，另一面凸起一浮雕人首，其形为立目，双眉呈"V"字形上挑，直鼻，高鼻梁，鼻孔外翻。口前噘，下颌较平，面颊高凸。双眉间额头与头顶呈凸弧面形。樽表面饰压地方格纹，底面略上凹。樽内壁磨制光滑。樽盖呈球冠状，其上端有一桥钮，表面饰压地方格纹，其内边缘有一圈凸棱与樽体配合。此樽造型规整，装饰奇特，工艺难度大，水平高。此樽属马家窑文化型，以方格表示连山纹，器表之人面像当是炎帝之本相。

图 3.32 饰人首带盖樽（马家窑文化）

Figure 3.32 Zun decorated with a human image (Majiayao culture)

3.32 Zun Decorated with a Human Image（Majiayao Culture）（Figure 3.32）

Height: 18 cm, belly width: 9 cm, maximum width: 13.2 cm, base diameter: 5.2 cm, mouth diameter: 5.5 cm, weight: 1160 g, volume: 280 mL.

It is made of sapphire with corrosive brownish red markings and spots.

The upper part of the Zun is bulged, the lower getting thin, and the mouth rim contracted, so formed the fold shoulder and bulged belly. The bottom is slightly concave, and the surface and inner wall were polished smooth. There is a bridge-shaped button with a flat round hole on one side of the belly, and the other side is decorated with a high relief human head, whose shape is sloping up eyes, V-shaped eyebrows, high nose bridge, turning out nostrils, mouth pouted, flat chin, high convex cheeks, and the top of the head is in convex surface shape. The surface of the Zun was decorated with embossed square lattice patterns. The lid is convex with a bridge-shaped button, and decorated with square lattice patterns. There is a circle of convex edge along the inner edge for matching the mouth of the body. The Zun is in well balance with peculiar shape and difficult technical process, and it is high-level jade work. It is in Majiayao cultural type. The square lattice patterns stand for the continued-mountain marks of the Emperor Yan Clan, and the human head image decorated on the surface should be the Emperor Yan image.

3.33 双口瓶 (小河沿文化) (图 3.33)

高 12.2 cm，宽 14.8 cm，厚 9.7 cm，重 2000 g，容积 120 mL。

熊胆青玉，棕、红沁色，有灰皮、蚀纹及漆状亮斑。

瓶体呈椭球形，平底，上端两瓶颈并列，瓶颈高 3.8 cm，瓶口外径 4 cm，内径 3 cm。瓶内壁呈球面形且互相连通，磨制光滑。瓶外侧有三对桥形凸钮，钮中间有对钻孔，孔两侧有斜槽。此双口瓶外型美观、规整，加工难度大，工艺水平高。此双口瓶与 1977 年赤峰市大南沟墓地出土的一件陶制双口瓶形同，该陶瓶属小河沿文化型。

图 3.33　双口瓶(小河沿文化)

Figure 3.33　Dual-nozzle bottle (Xiaoheyan culture)

3.33 Dual-nozzle Bottle (Xiaoheyan Culture) (Figure 3.33)

Height: 12.2 cm, width: 14.8 cm, thickness: 9.7 cm, weight: 2000 g, volume: 120 mL.

It is made of bile-colored jade with brownish red markings and lacquer-like spots.

The body of the bottle is in ellipsoid shape with flat base, with a pair of vertical bottle necks on the top. Its inner wall is in spherical shape and ground smooth, where the two necks are connected each other inside. There are three pairs of buttons on the surface, each button with a drilling hole. This dual-nozzle bottle looks neat, and with difficult technical process. Its shape is the same as the Xiaoheyan cultural pottery dual-nozzle bottle unearthed from Danangou cemetery. Chifeng City in 1977.

3.34　鬶（山东龙山文化）（图 3.34）

高 20 cm，长 18 cm，宽 9.5 cm，重 3100 g。

白石质，其中有金属颗粒，表面有金属亮点，稍有透明度，有灰皮、蚀斑、浅棕红沁色，石声清悠。

鬶体前宽后窄，鬶口直立呈喇叭口形，口内有一直槽，未深入到体内。管口前方有舌形流，其内壁呈折叶形。鬶有三袋足，前二后一，两前足粗壮，后足短小略内弯。底面平光，上部圆隆，自前至后以剔地法饰出三层覆甲，覆甲边缘上翻，并且饰对称减地乳丁纹。提梁似兽尾，自覆甲之末端上弯至鬶口之颈后，其上饰剔地"人"字形绳纹。提梁后端呈"人"字形与覆甲边缘相连。此鬶造型美观、规整，工艺水平极高。山东龙山文化有类似的陶鬶。

3.34　Ritual Device—Gui（Shandong Longshan Culture）（Figure 3.34）

Height: 20 cm, length: 18 cm, width: 9.5 cm, weight: 3100 g.

It is made of white stone with corrosive light brownish red and gray skin, slightly translucent, and with metal particles which formed many shiny points on surface, and with elegant percussion.

Gui is a water or wine container, which is a kind of ritual device. The shape of this Gui is similar to the flask showed in Figure 3.30, but the body of this one is longer. The upper body is convex with three layers of armor-shaped covers and decorated with bas-relief symmetric nipple patterns. The lifting beam looks like an animal tail and is decorated with V-shaped corrugates. This Gui is in beautiful shape and well-balanced, whose technology level is very high. The similar pottery Gui devices were found in the Shandong Longshan cultural sites.

图 3.34　鬶（山东龙山文化）

Figure 3.34　Ritual device—Gui
(Shandong Longshan culture)

C 其他类型的龙山文化玉器

这一部分玉器均属龙山文化类型,其中包括大汶口文化、山东龙山文化、陕西龙山文化、河南龙山文化等。器型包括人物头像、璧、环、圭、璇玑、斧、钺、钩形器、钩云纹佩、男根和羽人等造型。从这些玉器的造型和工艺可看出,其中有些是泛红山文化玉器的直接继承,如人物头像(图3.35)、璇玑(图3.40)、钩云形佩等;有些是受到良渚文化的影响,如琮形璧、兽面纹饰等。凸内缘璧是外星飞行器的造型(图3.47),璧与羽人的组合造型表示天外来客(图3.45、图3.46),这些都是外星生命崇拜的造型。龙山文化时期已从氏族公社过渡到中央集权,这一时期玉制的斧、钺、戚等兵器形礼器较多。图3.52是一件十分精美的玉戚。

C Other Types of Longshan Cultural Jade Works

This part of jade belongs to Longshan cultural type, including Dawenkou culture, Shandong Longshan culture, Shaanxi Longshan culture, Henan Longshan culture, etc. The shapes of jade pieces include human portraits, weapon-shaped ritual ornaments, ornaments related to reproduction culture, and jade accessories related to the UFO and aliens, etc. Some of them were the direct inheritance of Pan-Hongshan culture, such as the Bi, Xuanji, cloud-shaped wear, etc.; some were influenced by Liangzhu culture, such as Cong, animal mask and so on. The Bi with convex inner edge is a kind of alien spacecraft—UFO, shown in Figure 3.47; and the Bi combined with winged-angels is a kind of alien who came from the sky, shown in Figures 3.45, 3.46. This type of jade showed the alien worship of primitive religion. During the Longshan culture period, the nature of regime had been converted from the clan commune to the centralized monarchy, so more weapon-shaped ritual jade devices occurred. The Qi showed in Figure 3.52 is a very fine jade work.

3.35　人头像（陕西龙山文化）（图 3.35）

图中的两人头像造型与纹饰相同。

左：高 5.1 cm，宽 4.3 cm，厚 1.2 cm。

青玉，红、黑沁色，有灰皮。

右：高 5.3 cm，宽 4.6 cm，厚 1.2 cm。

青白玉，血丝纹沁色，有灰皮。

造型为一片状侧视人头像，鼻、口部凸起于边缘的一侧，另一侧凸起一耳。前额圆凸，双目位于两侧，接近头顶，呈枣核形，以阴刻线饰出。头顶有一椭圆形发髻，面颊部有一对钻圆孔，颈部也以一椭圆形凸块饰之。

此类头像源于泛红山文化玉作，本书图 1.12 中的人头像即是它们的原型，其造型与工艺均优于这两件。这两件人头像与 1979 年陕西神木石峁遗址出土的一件人头像形同，应属陕西龙山文化玉器。

图 3.35　人头像（陕西龙山文化）

Figure 3.35　Human image pendants（Shaanxi Longshan culture）

3.35 Human Image Pendants (Shaanxi Longshan Culture) (Figure 3.35)

These are two human head image pendants with the same shape and decorations.

(1) Left one

Height: 5.1 cm, width: 4.3 cm, thickness: 1.2 cm.

It is made of sapphire with corrosive black and red markings and gray spots.

(2) Right one

Height: 5.3 cm, width: 4.6 cm, thickness: 1.2 cm.

It is made of light green jade with corrosive bloodshot markings and gray spots.

The shape of the pendant is a side-looking human head image. The shape of the image is nose and mouth protruding at one side of the edge, and an ear protruding at the other side of edge; round and convex forehead, intaglio date kernel-shaped eyes on both sides near the top of head, an oval-shaped bun on the top of the head, a drilling hole on the cheek, and an oval-shaped pedestal at the neck position.

This type of the human head image originated from the Pan-Hongshan cultural jade, and the head image showed in Figure 1.12 was its prototype, whose shape and techniques were much better than these two. These two pieces of human images are the same as the jade human head image which was unearthed from Shimao site, Shenmu County, Shaanxi Province in 1979, so they should be Shaanxi Longshan cultural jade works.

3.36 钺(一)(大汶口文化)(图 3.36)

长 10 cm，末端宽 4 cm，刃宽 6.3 cm，厚 0.8 cm。

青玉，棕、红、黄等沁色，有灰皮。

钺之刃部呈凸弧形，肩部平直，两端为圆角。近肩部中央有一对钻圆孔，孔内有台阶。此钺与 1959 年山东泰安大汶口遗址出土的一件白色石钺形似，故属大汶口文化型玉器。

3.36 Yue—1 (Dawenkou Culture) (Figure 3.36)

Length: 10 cm, blade width: 6.3 cm, shoulder width: 4 cm, thickness: 0.8 cm.

It is made of sapphire with corrosive brown, red and yellow, etc. markings and gray spots.

The shape of the Yue is convex arc blade, straight shoulder with round corners, a funnel-shaped drilling hole at the center near the shoulder, which is drilled from both sides and with the drilling marks on its wall. This Yue is similar to the white stone Yue which was unearthed from Dawenkou site, Tai'an County, Shandong Province in 1959, so it should be the Dawenkou cultural jade work.

图 3.36　钺(一)(大汶口文化)

Figure 3.36　Yue—1 (Dawenkou culture)

图 3.37　铖(二)(大汶口文化)

Figure 3.37　Yue—2 (Dawenkou culture)

3.37　铖(二)(大汶口文化)(图 3.37)

长 9.7 cm，刃宽 5.5 cm，肩宽 3.8 cm，最厚 0.5 cm。

青玉，质优，棕、红沁色，有蚀斑及冰裂纹，玉声清脆。

此铖刃部与肩部均呈凸弧形，其刃部呈钝刃状，周边均有倒角。近肩部中央有一对钻圆孔。此铖造型规整，磨光度高。此铖具有大汶口文化玉铖特征，属大汶口文化玉器。

3.37　Yue—2 (Dawenkou Culture)(Figure 3.37)

Length: 9.7 cm, blade width: 5.5 cm, shoulder width: 3.8 cm, maximum thickness: 0.5 cm.

It is made of sapphire with corrosive brownish red markings and spots, ice crack-like motifs, and with elegant percussion.

The shape of the Yue is both of the blade and shoulder are in convex arc shape with blunt blade. The periphery was chamfered. There is a drilling hole at the center near the shoulder, and it was drilled from both sides. This Yue is well-balanced, and with highly polishing. It has the characteristics of the Dawenkou cultural jade Yue, so it should be the Dawenkou cultural jade piece.

3.38 钺（山东龙山文化）（图 3.38）

高 6.3 cm，刃宽 4.7 cm，肩宽 3.7 cm，最厚 0.7 cm。
青玉，棕色沁色，有蚀斑、蚀孔。

钺之轮廓呈圆角梯形，周边均有倒角。近肩部中央垂直方向有两圆孔，上小下大。此钺造型规整，磨光度高。这类周边减薄、四角抹圆、有两孔的玉钺多属大汶口文化或山东龙山文化玉器。

3.38 Yue（Shandong Longshan Culture）（Figure 3.38）

Height: 6.3 cm, blade width: 4.7 cm, shoulder width: 3.7 cm, maximum thickness: 0.7 cm.

It is made of sapphire with corrosive brown markings and spots.

The Yue is in trapezoidal shape with round corners and chamfered edges. There are two drilling holes along the central vertical direction near the shoulder, and the lower one is bigger and the upper one smaller. This Yue is well-balanced and with highly polishing. Most of this kind of Yue with chamfered edges, smooth corners and two holes belong to Dawenkou cultural jade or Shandong Longshan cultural jade.

图 3.38 钺（山东龙山文化）

Figure 3.38   Yue (Shandong Longshan culture)

3.39　斧（河南龙山文化）（图 3.39）

高 5.3 cm，刃宽 5.3 cm，最厚 1.1 cm。

青白玉，棕、黑沁色，色泽如漆，有灰皮。

轮廓呈梯形，刃部呈钝刀状，周边倒角呈圆角。肩部有一弧形凹槽，近肩部中央有一对钻圆孔，孔内有台阶。此斧与 1976 年河南孟津小潘沟出土的一绿松石斧形同，属河南龙山文化玉器（参看《中国玉器全集 1》图 49）。

图 3.39　斧（河南龙山文化）

Figure 3.39　Ax（Henan Longshan culture）

3.39　Ax（Henan Longshan Culture）（Figure 3.39）

Height: 5.3 cm, blade width: 5.3 cm, maximum thickness: 1.1 cm.

It is made of light green jade with corrosive black and brown markings and lacquer luster.

The ax is in trapezoidal shape with smooth corners, straight blunt blade and chamfered edges, a curved groove on the shoulder, and a bifacial drilling hole on the middle near the shoulder with the drilling marks inside the hole. This ax is the same as the turquoise ax unearthed from Xiaopangou site, Mengjin County, Henan Province in 1976, so it belongs to the relic of Henan Longshan culture（see *The Complete Works of Chinese Jade*, *Volume 1*, Figure 49）.

3.40 璇玑（山东龙山文化）（图 3.40）

直径 8 cm，孔径 3 cm，最厚 0.4 cm。

青玉，全沁呈棕、红色，有灰皮、蚀斑。

此璇玑中间厚，边缘薄，其横断面呈"V"字形。璇玑外缘均匀分布三个脊牙，每两牙之间饰三个凸块，每一凸块上饰三个锯齿形牙。此璇玑造型规整，磨制精细，属同类玉器之精品。此璇玑与 1977 年山东滕县里庄出土的一件璇玑形似，工艺也相同，属山东龙山文化玉作。

璇玑源于泛红山文化时期，龙山文化璇玑是其继承，但工艺特点不同（《红山文化玉记》图 1.112）。

3.40 Xuanji Disc（Shandong Longshan Culture）（Figure 3.40）

Diameter: 8 cm, aperture: 3 cm, maximum thickness: 0.4 cm.

It is made of sapphire with corrosive brownish red markings and spots.

The surface of Xuanji is convex, and the edge was chamfered. There are three cantilevers evenly distributed on the outer edge, and three bumps on each cantilever, and three teeth were decorated on each bump. This Xuanji is well-balanced, and with highly polishing. It is the fine piece among the same kind of Xuanji pieces. It is similar to the jade Xuanji unearthed from Li Village, Teng County, Shan-dong Province in 1977, and with the same technique process, so it belongs to Shandong Longshan cultural jade.

The Longshan cultural Xuanji was the continuation of the Pan-Hongshan cultural Xuanji, but in different technological process（Figure 1.112 in *The Hongshan Cultural Jade Records*）.

图 3.40 璇玑（山东龙山文化）

Figure 3.40 Xuanji disc (Shandong Longshan culture)

3.41　璇玑（泛红山文化）（图 3.41）

直径 6 cm，孔径 3.2 cm，最厚 1.3 cm。

熊胆青玉，棕、红沁色，有灰皮，蜡状光泽。

此璇玑外缘呈方圆形，内外缘均倒角，横断面呈橄榄形。四角各有一凸脊，每一凸脊上有三齿，其形似蝉。此璇玑的造型与工艺均属泛红山文化型玉器，放在这里是为了便于比较。

图 3.41　璇玑（泛红山文化）

Figure 3.41　Xuanji disc（Pan-Hongshan culture）

3.41　Xuanji Disc（Pan-Hongshan Culture）（Figure 3.41）

Diameter: 6 cm, aperture: 3.2 cm, maximum thickness: 1.3 cm.

It is made of bile-colored jade with corrosive brownish red markings and waxy luster.

There are four cantilevers evenly distributed on the outer edge, and with three teeth on each cantilever. It seems to be a prone cicada on each cantilever. The cross-section is in olive shape. It is Pan-Hongshan cultural type jade work, placed here for easier comparison.

3.42　舌形玉斧（江淮地区原始文化）（图 3.42）

高 7.6 cm，上宽 5 cm，最厚 1.5 cm 。

黄玉，表面有灰皮、蚀斑、蚀孔及融化现象。

斧呈舌形，底端平直，有两圆孔形槽，近端部中央有一对钻直孔。斧之两面均饰兽面纹，其形为卵形立目，直鼻，鼻孔外翻，鼻翼两侧各饰一逗号形云纹，口部上弯。纹饰以浅浮雕饰出。因表面融化，纹饰不清晰。舌形斧曾发现于北阴阳营文化遗址，此玉斧可能属江淮地区原始文化玉作。

3.42　Tongue-shaped Ax（Jianghuai Primitive Culture）（Figure 3.42）

Height: 7.6 cm, shoulder width: 5 cm, maximum thickness: 1.5 cm.

It is made of topaz with corrosive light brown skin, spots and melting phenomenon.

This ax is in tongue shape, with shoulder flat, two round grooves, and a straight drilling hole on the center near the shoulder. A pair of animal masks was decorated on both sides. Its shape is sloping up oval eyes, straight nose bridge, turning out nostrils. The comma-shaped motifs are decorated on both sides of the nose with concave arc-shaped mouth. The motifs were decorated with bas-relief technique. Due to the surface melting, the decorations are not clear. The tongue-shaped ax was found in Beiyinyangying cultural site, so this ax may be the relic of Jianghuai primitive culture.

图 3.42　舌形玉斧（江淮地区原始文化）

Figure 3.42　Tongue-shaped Ax (Jianghuai primitive culture)

3.43　兽面纹璧（江淮地区原始文化）（图 3.43）

直径 8 cm，孔径 2 cm，最厚 1.7 cm。

黄玉，棕色沁色，有蚀斑、蚀孔，表面有融化现象。

此璧两面呈凸弧形隆起，两面纹饰相同。以直径为轴饰两个对称的璜，以减地法饰出边界纹，在每一璜上饰一兽面纹，纹饰以浅浮雕及压地法饰出。兽面形为双目呈曲边四边形，内眼角相连，双目间呈"V"字形，其上端有一道横向凸弦纹，形成一个倒三角形连桥，睛珠圆凸。此璧的玉质、纹饰与技法均与图 3.42 相似，属同一类文化玉器。此璧的造型与图 2.32 中的良渚文化玉璧也有类似之处，表明两地间有文化交流。

3.43　Bi Disc Decorated with Animal Mask Motifs（Jianghuai Primitive Culture）（Figure 3.43）

Diameter: 8 cm, aperture: 2 cm, maximum thickness: 1.7 cm.

It is made of topaz with corrosive brown skin, spots and melting phenomenon.

It is in convex surface and with the same decorations on both sides. A pair of symmetrical bas-relief Huang was decorated on each side, and an animal mask was decorated on each Huang. Its shape is curved quadrilateral-shaped eyes with convex round eye beads, inside eye corners connected, and an inverted isosceles triangle pattern was decorated between the eyes. The material, decoration and technique of this Bi are similar to the ax showed in Figure 3.42; they belong to the same kind of cultural jade. This Bi is also similar to the Liangzhu cultural Bi disc showed in Figure 2.32, and it indicated the cultural exchanging between Jianghuai cultural district and Liangzhu cultural district.

图 3.43　兽面纹璧（江淮地区原始文化）

Figure 3.43　Bi disc decorated with animal mask matifs (Jianghuai primitive culture)

3.44 环（大汶口文化）（图 3.44）

外径 20 cm，内径 9.3 cm，厚 0.7 cm。

黄玉，全沁呈棕、红色，表面侵蚀较重，有灰皮、蚀斑及蚀孔。

环的中心孔略偏向一侧，其内壁磨制光滑。此环与 1987 年江苏省新沂县花厅村出土的一环形似，属大汶口文化型玉器。

图 3.44 环（大汶口文化）

Figure 3.44 Ring（Dawenkou culture）

3.44 Ring（Dawenkou Culture）（Figure 3.44）

Outer diameter: 20 cm, inner diameter: 9.3 cm, thickness: 0.7 cm.

It is made of topaz with corrosive brownish red markings, gray spots and pits.

The central hole slightly deviats to one side, and the surfaces of the ring are flat and polished smooth. This ring is similar to the ring unearthed from Huating site, Xinyi County, Jiangsu Province in 1987. It is the relic of Dawenkou culture.

3.45 饰羽人出廓璧(一)(龙山文化)(图3.45)

直径4.3 cm,最大直径5.3 cm,孔径1.2 cm,最厚1.1 cm。全沁呈棕色,包浆厚重,有蚀斑、蚀孔,蜡状光泽。

璧之两面呈凸弧面,中间厚,内外边缘薄。璧之外缘均匀饰有三个带翼羽人,羽人趴伏于璧缘。羽人形为鸟首人身,背上有翼。双目圆凸,尖喙。下颔紧贴于璧之外缘,四肢紧贴于璧上,形象生动。此造型实为先民对天外来客及其飞行器的艺术表现,它使我们了解到,古人说的羽人即是指天外来客。此璧内外缘减薄的制作方法显然受到泛红山文化的影响,但人物的表现技法不同,可能属龙山文化玉器。

3.45 Bi Disc Decorated with Feathered Angels—1 (Longshan Culture) (Figure 3.45)

Diameter: 4.3 cm, maximum diameter: 5.3 cm, aperture: 1.2 cm, maximum thickness: 1.1 cm.

It was covered with corrosive brown skin and spots, and waxy luster on the surface.

The surfaces of the Bi are convex, and the outer and inner edges are chamfered. Three same-shaped prone feathered angels were evenly distributed on the outer edge. The shape of the angel is bird head and human body with wing on its back, round convex eyes, acuminate beak, chin close to the edge, limbs attached to the Bi. The shape is vivid. In fact, it is the artistic expression of the extraterrestrials and their vehicles, which makes us aware that the so-called "feathered angel" actually means the extraterrestrial. The shape of this Bi is clearly influenced by the Pan-Hongshan cultural jade works, but the characters of performance techniques are different, so it may be the relic of Longshan culture.

图3.45 饰羽人出廓璧(一)(龙山文化)

Figure 3.45 Bi disc decorated with feathered angels—1 (Longshan culture)

3.46　饰羽人出廓璧(二)（龙山文化）（图 3.46）

直径 5.1 cm，最大直径 7.5 cm，孔径 1.6 cm，厚 0.8 cm。

青玉，棕、红沁色，有蚀斑。

璧之两面均呈凸弧面，中间厚，内外边缘薄。璧之外缘均匀分布四个羽人，它们的间隔为 90°。羽人趴伏于璧之外缘，仰头，弓背，圆形双目，上肢前伸，身体有羽毛覆盖。每一个羽人双臂下方有一对钻圆孔。此玉饰的寓意与图 3.45 相同。

图 3.46　饰羽人出廓璧(二)（龙山文化）

Figure 3.46　Bi disc decorated with feathered angels—2（Longshan culture）

3.46　Bi Disc Decorated with Feathered Angels—2（Longshan Culture）（Figure 3.46）

Diameter: 5.1 cm, maximum diameter: 7.5 cm, aperture: 1.6 cm, thickness: 0.8 cm.

It is made of sapphire with corrosive brownish red markings and spots.

The surfaces of the Bi are convex; the outer and inner edges are chamfered. Four same-shaped prone feathered angels are evenly distributed on the outer edge. They are in same shape, round eyes looking upward, arched back, upper limbs reaching, body covered with feathers, a drilling hole under its arms. The moral of this Bi is the same as the Bi showed in Figure 3.45.

3.47　凸内缘方圆形璧（龙山文化）（图 3.47）

射径（对角线长）6.7 cm，内径 2.3 cm，厚 0.4 cm，凸内缘高 0.8 cm。

青玉，棕、红沁色，有灰皮、蚀斑。

方圆形璧始于泛红山文化，此璧也是方圆形，但边缘减薄不够。凸内缘璧始于新石器时期，多见于商代，特别是广汉文化玉器中。此璧顶视呈琮形，也可称琮形璧。此璧也是外星飞行器的形状，可能是龙山文化玉器。此璧造型规整，地子平，磨光度好。

图 3.47　凸内缘方圆形璧（龙山文化）

Figure 3.47　Square-round Bi disc with convex inner edge（Longshan culture）

3.47　Square-round Bi Disc with Convex Inner Edge （Longshan Culture）（Figure 3.47）

Diagonal: 6.7 cm, aperture: 2.3 cm, thickness: 0.4 cm, height of inner edge: 0.8 cm.

It is made of sapphire with corrosive brownish red markings and spots.

This kind of Bi with protruding inner edge, began in the Neolithic period, more prevalent in the Shang Dynasty, especially in the Guanghan cultural jade. The top view of this Bi is in Cong shape, so also known as Cong-shaped Bi. In fact, it is the shape of alien spacecraft. This Bi is well-balanced, and the surface is highly polished.

3.48　琮形璧（龙山文化）（图 3.48）

此璧轮廓呈正方形，边长 4.5 cm，孔径 1.1 cm，厚 0.5 cm。

青玉，棕、红沁色，色泽很美，有蚀斑、蚀孔。

造型为正方形片状，中心有一圆孔，两面以圆孔为中心各饰一圆台，以减地法饰出，这样即形成了琮端部的形象。此璧表面尚留有开片时的割痕与减地时的磨制痕，属龙山文化玉作。

图 3.48　琮形璧（龙山文化）

Figure 3.48　Cong-shaped Bi disc（Longshan culture）

3.48　Cong-shaped Bi Disc（Longshan Culture）（Figure 3.48）

Side length: 4.5 cm, aperture: 1.1 cm, thickness: 0.5 cm.

It is made of sapphire with corrosive brownish red markings and spots.

Its shape is just as a top view of a Cong, which is the so-called Cong-shaped Bi, with the square-shape base and a relief round ring on the center. It was carved on both sides with the same shape. The cutting and grinding marks were still left on the surfaces. It is the relic of Longshan culture.

3.49　钩云纹佩（龙山文化）（图 3.49）

图中两佩的造型、纹饰与工艺皆相同。

左：佩略呈圆形，最大直径 5.8 cm，厚 0.7 cm。

青玉，有灰皮、蚀斑及蚀纹。

右：最大直径 5.8 cm，厚 0.6 cm。

青玉，棕色沁色，有灰皮、蚀斑及蚀纹。

佩为片状双面雕，两面纹饰相同，中央镂空呈倒钩形，其上饰瓦沟纹。钩下端边缘处有一对钻孔。边缘外侧在钩的顶端和两侧各饰一对牛角。此佩略似红山文化的云形佩，但制作工艺不同，属龙山文化玉器。

由于豕韦氏族的南迁，其玉文化也随之扩散到龙山文化区及良渚文化区，如钩云形佩、钩形器、玉鸮、方圆形璧等出现在龙山文化玉器中即是很有力的证明。

3.49　Moire Pendants（Longshan Culture）（Figure 3.49）

This is a pair of round moire pendants with the same shape and decoration.

（1）Left one

Maximum diameter: 5.8 cm, thickness: 0.7 cm.

It is made of sapphire with corrosive gray skin and pits.

（2）Right one

Maximum diameter: 5.8 cm, thickness: 0.6 cm.

It is made of sapphire with corrosive brown markings and pits.

It is plaque pendant, which is carved on both sides and decorated with the same motifs. It was hollowed with a hook on the center, and decorated with corrugate patterns on the hook. There are three pairs of horns decorated on the outer edge and distributed on the top and both sides. These pendants are similar to the Hongshan cultural cloud-shaped ornaments, but in different techniques. They belong to Longshan cultural jade pieces.

As Shiwei Clan migrated southward, their jade culture subsequently spread to the Longshan cultural district and Liangzhu cultural district. The strong proof about the fact is that many Hongshan cultural jade works appeared in the Longshan cultural district, such as the hook-shaped moire pendant, hook-shaped ornaments, jade owl pendants, square-round shaped Bi and so on.

图 3.49　勾云纹佩（龙山文化）

Figure 3.49　Moire pendants (Longshan Culture)

3.50　男根（龙山文化）（图 3.50）

长 5.5 cm，根部宽 2.7 cm，厚 1.3 cm。

绿松石，棕、红沁色，有蚀斑。

造型为一男性生殖器，根部为一对睾丸，其上饰多重回纹，两睾丸间有一"V"字形槽。阴茎饰有六道瓦沟纹，龟头为半圆形，前端有一桥形钮，中间有一圆孔。根部断面有一弧形槽。此玉饰与第一册《红山文化玉记》中图 1.113"兽面蛹片饰"形似，证明该兽面蛹也有男根的寓意。二者都是男根的艺术表现形式。

3.50　Male Genital Pendant （Longshan Culture）（Figure 3.50）

Length: 5.5 cm, maximum width: 2.7 cm, thickness: 1.3 cm.

It is made of turquoise with corrosive brownish red markings and spots.

The pendant is in male genital modeling. Its shape is a pair of testicles at the end decorated with multi-fret patterns, a V-shaped gap between the two testicles, and a curved groove on the top. Six lateral grooves were decorated on the penis. The glans is in semi-circle shape and a bridge-shaped button with a round hole is on the middle. This ornament is similar to the ornament showed in Figure 1.113 " Pupa Pendant " in *The Hongshan Cultural Jade Records*, which proves that the pupa pendant has the same moral of male genital. Both of them are the artistic forms of male genital.

图 3.50　男根（龙山文化）

Figure 3.50　Male genital pendant
(Longshan culture)

3.51 圭（山东龙山文化）（图 3.51）

长 10.4 cm，上宽 4 cm，下宽 3.5 cm，厚 0.8 cm。

青玉，棕红沁色，沁色呈斑块形及丝纹形。

圭呈条形片状，上端略宽，两侧抹成斜角，尖端平齐，近末端有一对钻圆孔。圭之一面饰兽面纹，其形为重回纹大目，面颊下垂，云纹鼻，尖折形口，额头饰云纹。兽面上方有两组平行带状纹，每一带上有两道瓦沟纹。反面饰有两道贯穿前后的纵向凹槽，以打洼法饰出。

此圭的造型与纹饰都有生殖文化的寓意。此圭外形是男性阴茎的形状，其上的兽面纹即是男性生殖器，双目是睾丸，面部是阴茎和包皮，尖状的口是龟头。此兽面纹的外形也似一只展翅的飞鸟，鸟也有男根的寓意。值得注意的是，在龙山文化与良渚文化中皆以多重回纹表示睾丸。1969 年山东省日照市两城镇出土一玉锛，其上纹饰与此件相似，当属同时期的作品。

3.51 Gui（Shandong Longshan Culture）（Figure 3.51）

Length: 10.4 cm, width: 3.5—4 cm, thickness: 0.8 cm.
It is made of sapphire with brownish red markings.

The Gui is a strip-shaped plaque with slightly taper. It has trapezoidal-shaped top and flat rear edge. One side of the Gui was decorated with animal mask, whose shape is multi-fret big eyes, sagging cheeks, curled nose, angular mouth, forehead with moire patterns. There are two parallel strips above the mask, and decorated with corrugations on each strip. The other side of the Gui were decorated with two longitudinal grooves. There is a bifacial drilling hole on the middle near the rear edge.

Both of its shape and decoration have the connotation of the reproductive culture. Its contour is in male penis shape. The animal mask stands for the male genital, and the animal eyes stand for the testicles. The face stands for the penis and foreskin, and the angular tip stands for the glans. The contour of the mask also looks like a flying bird; the bird has the moral of male genital, too. It is noteworthy that both in the Longshan cultural jade and Liangzhu cultural jade, the multi-fret patterns stand for the male testicles. The decoration on this Gui is similar to the decoration on an adze which was unearthed from the site of Liangcheng Town, Rizhao City, Shandong Province in 1969, so they should be in the same period.

图 3.51 圭（山东龙山文化）

Figure 3.51 Gui (Shandong Longshan culture)

3.52 戚（神木石峁文化）（图 3.52）

高 14.5 cm，刃宽 10 cm，肩宽 7.8 cm，最厚 0.6 cm，重 220 g。

黄玉，质优，棕、黄沁色，有灰皮与赭色蚀斑。

戚纵断面呈楔形，刃部呈凸弧形，尖端平齐，两侧为凹弧形。每侧凸起三个水滴状凸脊，与援部相接处有减地台阶。援部上方有一单面钻漏斗孔。戚之两面均有开片时留下的割痕。

此戚玉质优良，造型美观，磨光度好，属神木石峁玉器之上品。台北故宫博物院与陕西博物馆均有类似的神木石峁玉戚。

3.52 Qi Pendant（Shenmu Shimao Culture）（Figure 3.52）

Height: 14.5 cm, blade width: 10 cm, shoulder width: 7.8 cm, maximum thickness: 0.6 cm, weight: 220 g.

It is made of high-quality topaz with corrosive brownish yellow markings and lacquer-like bright purple spots.

The vertical section of the Qi is in wedge shape, which has convex arc-shaped blade, concave-shaped side edges and flat shoulder. There are three drop-shaped ridges on each side, and a funnel-shaped drilling hole on the middle near the shoulder. There are cutting marks on both sides.

The Qi is in beautiful shape and with highly polishing. It is top-grade jade among the Shenmu Shimao cultural jade. The similar jade Qi pieces were collected in Taipei's National Palace Museum and Shaanxi Museum.

图 3.52 戚（神木石峁文化）

Figure 3.52 Qi pendant (Shenmu Shimao culture)

3.53　钩形器（龙山文化）（图 3.53）

长 8.5 cm，宽 4.5 cm，最厚 1.1 cm。

青玉，棕、灰沁色，有灰皮、蚀斑。

此器为片状，周边倒角似双面刃。一面呈波纹状，另一面呈双钩状。中间有乳突状凸脊，其上饰两道弦纹。在器之一面凸棱的上方饰一兽面纹，其形为环形双目，其间有拱形连桥，扁方形口。纹饰以压地法饰出。钩之上缘有一对钻孔。

此器的外形与红山文化玉钩形器形似，其上的兽面纹与良渚简化兽面纹相同，兼具南北两种风格，属龙山文化玉作。

图 3.53　钩形器（龙山文化）

Figure 3.53　Hook-shaped pendant（Longshan culture）

3.53　Hook-shaped Pendant（Longshan Culture）（Figure 3.53）

Length: 8.5 cm, width: 4.5 cm, maximum thickness: 1.1 cm.

It is made of sapphire with corrosive brownish gray markings and spots.

It is a plaque pendant. The peripheral edges were chamfered, which seems to be double-edged blade. One edge is in ripple shape, and the other edge is in double-hook shape with a papillary ridge on the middle and two intaglio short lines. There is an animal mask decorated on one side above the ridge, and its shape is glasses-shaped eyes, flat rectangular-shaped mouth, and the motifs were decorated with embossing technique.

The shape of the pendant is similar to the hook-shaped pendant of Hongshan cultural jade, and the animal mask is the same as Liangzhu simplified animal mask. It has both north and south jade styles, which is the characteristic of the Longshan cultural jade.

3.54　兽牙形器（大汶口文化）（图 3.54）

长 13 cm，末端宽 5.2 cm，最厚 0.8 cm。

黄玉，全沁呈棕、黄色，有灰皮、蚀斑及蚀孔。

器呈片状獠牙形，一面打磨平光，另一面厚度不一，部分表面保持自然形态，可能是由一玉石的边料所制。末端两角各有一对钻孔。此器造型古朴，可能是大汶口文化玉器，考古发掘证明大汶口文化墓地出土的獠牙形器最多。

图 3.54　兽牙形器（大汶口文化）

Figure 3.54　Tusk-shaped pendant（Dawenkou Culture）

3.54　Tusk-shaped Pendant（Dawenkou Culture）（Figure 3.54）

Length: 13 cm, shoulder width: 5.2 cm, maximum thickness: 0.8 cm.

It is made of topaz with corrosive brownish yellow markings and spots.

It is a plaque pendant in tusk shape. One side of it is ground flat, and a part of surface on the other side keep the natural status, which may be subject to material restrictions. Its upper part of the step is ground flat, and its lower part was kept in natural and only polished smooth. There are two drilling holes on both sides near the shoulder. This pendant has ancient manners, which may be Dawenkou cultural jade work. Archaeological excavations proved that most of the tusk-shaped pendants were unearthed from the Dawenkou cultural cemeteries.

D 其他地区的新石器时期文化玉器

这一部分玉器包括了江淮地区原始文化玉器、北阴阳营文化玉器、凌家滩文化玉器、石峡文化玉器、卑南文化玉器、齐家文化玉器、仰韶文化玉器和二里头文化玉器等，其中有人物、璧、琮、璋、珠、斧、钺、刀、铲、戚等。由此可知，这些玉器中的很多造型或纹饰受到泛红山文化和良渚文化的影响，例如其中的两件人物造像（图 3.66、图 3.67）为凌家滩型女子造型，与卑南型男子造型均受到泛红山文化的影响。江淮地区的玉璧、玉钺等造型则是受到良渚文化的影响。这些地区的玉器有些也是十分精美的，如图 3.61 是一件体量大、玉质好、制作精美的北阴阳营七孔玉刀，图 3.62 也是一件新石器时期早期的精美舌形玉斧。仰韶文化的玉器不多，图 3.72 是一件制作精美的仰韶文化有肩玉钺。图 3.73 是一件十分有创意的仰韶文化陶制男祖形鼠。

D The Neolithic Cultural Jade Works of Other Cultural Regions

This part of jade includes the primitive cultural jade works in Jianghuai region, Lingjiatan cultural jade works, Shixia cultural jade works, Beinan cultural jade works, Beiyinyangying cultural jade works, Yangshao cultural jade works and Erlitou cultural jade works, etc. There are Bi, Cong, beads, axes, Yue, knives, shovels and Qi, etc. among them. We can see that many modelings and decorotions among these jade works were influenced by Pan-Hongshan culture and Liangzhu culture, such as the two human figures, Figures 3.66 and 3.67, belong to the Lingjiatan cultural type of jade. Both Lingjiatan cultural type and Beinan cultural type are the inheritance of Pan-Hongshan cultural jade; the Bi, Yue, etc. in Jianghuai region were influenced by Liangzhu cultural jade works. Some of this part of jade are also very beautiful, such as Figure 3.61 is a large-size, good-quality, exquisite seven-hole knife, Figure 3.62 is an early Neolithic exquisite tongue-shaped ax. The quantity of jade is relatively small in Yangshao cultural region. Figure 3.72 is a beautiful shouldered ax; Figure 3.73 is a very innovative genitalia- shaped mouse. Both of them belong to Yangshao cultural relics.

3.55　钺（龙山文化）（图 3.55）

高 4 cm，刀宽 5.3 cm。

青玉，棕色沁色，有灰皮及冰裂纹。

造型为一不对称形钺，两面呈凸弧面，周边倒角。援部呈弯月形，内部偏向一端，呈弧边梯形状。内之端面平光，其上有一横向对钻孔。钺之两面均饰一兽面纹，其形为环形双目，直鼻，扁方形口，纹饰以浅浮雕饰出。此兽面纹与良渚简化兽面纹相似。其制作工艺又具红山文化风格，应属龙山文化玉器。这类不对称的钺也称靴形钺，它是古越族的图腾标志。

3.55　Yue Pendant （Longshan Culture）（Figure 3.55）

Height: 4 cm, blade width: 5.3 cm.

It is made of sapphire with corrosive brown markings and ice crack-shaped veins.

It is an asymmetric-shaped Yue with convex surface on both sides, and chamfered peripheral edges. Its body is in meniscus shape with a slant Nei. The Nei is in trapezoidal shape with concave sides and flat top, and there is an ox nostril-shaped drilling hole on the top. An animal mask were decorated on each side. Its shape is ring-shaped eyes, straight nose, flat rectangular-shaped mouth. The motifs were decorated with bas-relief technique. The animal mask is similar to the Liangzhu simplified animal mask. Its production process is similar to the Hongshan cultural jade style, so it should belong to Longshan cultural jade. This kind of asymmetric-shaped Yue, also known as boot-shaped Yue, is the totemic symbol of the ancient Yue ethnic.

图 3.55　钺（龙山文化）

Figure 3.55　Yue pendant (Longshan culture)

3.56　璧(一)(江淮地区原始文化)(图 3.56)

直径 6.4 cm, 孔径 1.1 cm, 厚 0.5 ~ 0.6 cm。

黄玉, 棕、红、灰等沁色, 有灰皮、蚀斑及蚀纹。

此璧制作古朴, 表面留有明显的磨制擦痕。中心孔为两面对钻, 因对中不准, 两面的孔各偏向一边, 因而出现明显的台阶。此璧当属新石器时期早期作品, 可能属江淮地区原始文化玉器。

图 3.56　璧(一)(江淮地区原始文化)

Figure 3.56　Bi disc—1 (Jianghuai primitive culture)

3.56　Bi Disc—1 (Jianghuai Primitive Culture)(Figure 3.56)

Diameter: 6.4 cm, aperture: 1.1 cm, thickness: 0.5—0.6 cm.

It is made of topaz with corrosive brown, red, gray, etc. markings and veins.

This Bi is in very old style, and obvious grinding scratches were left on surface. The central hole is drilled from both sides; the centers of the hole on both sides are not concentric, as a result an obvious step was left on the wall of the hole. It maybe belongs to Jianghuai primitive cultural jade.

3.57　璧（二）（江淮地区原始文化）（图 3.57）

直径 7.1 cm，孔径 1.8 cm，厚 0.4～0.5 cm。

湖绿玉，玉质温润，棕、灰沁色，有蚀斑、蚀纹。

此璧开片不均匀，薄厚不一。中心孔为一对钻孔，孔内有台阶。此璧为素璧，两面磨制平光。此璧玉质为湖绿玉，应属良渚文化或江淮地区原始文化玉器。

图 3.57　璧（二）（江淮地区原始文化）

Figure 3.57　Bi disc—2（Jianghuai primitive culture）

3.57　Bi Disc—2（Jianghuai Primitive Culture）（Figure 3.57）

Diameter: 7.1 cm, aperture: 1.8 cm, thickness: 0.4—0.5 cm.

It is made of lake-green jade with corrosive brownish gray markings and spots.

The cross-section is in taper shape. The central hole was drilled from both sides, and there is a step on the wall of the hole. Both sides of the surfaces of the Bi were plain and polished smooth. From the shape and material of view, this Bi should belong to Liangzhu or Jianghuai primitive cultural jade work.

3.58 璧（马家浜文化）（图 3.58）

图中两璧的玉质、沁色、造型与工艺相同。

左：直径 5.2 cm，孔径 1 cm，最厚 0.7 cm，边缘厚 0.3 cm。

右：直径 5.6 cm，孔径 1 cm，最厚 0.7 cm，边缘厚 0.3 cm。

青白玉，质优，有黑斑与棕色沁色。

璧之中间厚，边缘薄，断面呈梭形。中心孔为单面钻，孔呈漏斗形，孔壁磨光呈弧面。此璧两面均有开片时留下的割痕。磨光度很好。

马家浜文化玉璧、玉玦有与此璧类似的造型和工艺，此璧应属马家浜文化玉器。

图 3.58 璧（马家浜文化）

Figure 3.58 Bi discs（Majiabang culture）

3.58 Bi Discs（Majiabang Culture）（Figure 3.58）

The two pieces of Bi are with the same jade, corrosive colors, shape and technique process.
（1）Left one
Diameter: 5.2 cm, aperture: 1 cm, maximum thickness: 0.7 cm, edge thickness: 0.3 cm.
（2）Right one
Diameter: 5.6 cm, aperture: 1 cm, maximum thickness: 0.7 cm, edge thickness: 0.3 cm.
They are made of high-quality light green jade with corrosive brown and black markings.

Each of them is with convex surface on both sides, and chamfered peripheral edge. The central hole was drilled from one side in the funnel shape. The surface and the wall of the hole were polished smooth, and the cutting marks were left on the surface.

The shape and process of this Bi are similar to some of Majiabang cultural Bi and Jue, so it should belong to Majiabang cultural jade.

3.59 钺（良渚文化）（图 3.59）

高 9.5 cm，刃宽 8 cm，肩宽 6 cm，孔径 2.1 cm。

湖绿玉，有棕、红、黄等沁色及灰皮。

钺之轮廓呈梯形，刃部呈凸弧钝刃状，两侧倒角成圆角，肩部端面平齐，近肩部中央有一圆孔。此璧造型规整，磨光度好。此璧的玉质与造型均似良渚文化玉器，应属良渚文化型玉器。

图 3.59 钺（良渚文化）

Figure 3.59 Yue pendant（Liangzhu culture）

3.59 Yue Pendant（Liangzhu Culture）（Figure 3.59）

Height: 9.5 cm, blade width: 8 cm, shoulder width: 6 cm, aperture: 2.1 cm.

It is made of lake-green jade with brown, red, yellow markings and gray spots.

The contour of the Yue is in trapezoidal shape with a convex blunt blade. Both sides were chamfered, and the top of the shoulder is flat. This Yue is well-balanced, and highly polishing. Its jade and shape are similar to Liangzhu cultural jade works, so it should belong to Liangzhu cultural jade.

3.60 琮（石峡文化）（图 3.60）

高 4.1 cm，宽 7.2 cm，孔径 5.3 cm。

灰玉，棕、红沁色，有蚀斑、蚀纹，蜡状光泽。

琮呈扁方形，端面呈圆台形，两端面间有一直孔。此琮造型不够规整，上端面呈斜坡形。琮体外侧以四棱为中线各饰一神人面纹，其形为头戴宽带形羽冠，其上饰三道平行线纹，面部呈半圆形，下颏前翘，双目和口均为凹槽形，以打洼法饰出。琮之内壁磨制光滑。此琮的造型明显受到良渚文化的影响，但工艺水平相差很多。

图 3.60　琮（石峡文化）

Figure 3.60　Cong（Shixia culture）

3.60 Cong（Shixia Culture）（Figure 3.60）

Height: 4.1 cm, width: 7.2 cm, aperture: 5.3 cm.

It is made of gray jade with reddish brown markings and spots, and waxy luster.

This is a flat-square-shaped Cong. Its shape is a cylindrical tube with four right angle-shaped bumps evenly distributed around the surface. The Cong is not in balance, and sloping on the top. Four relief human faces were decorated on the four corner bumps, with the edges as the central axes, whose shape is wearing a board band-shaped crest with decorative parallel lines, semi-circle-shaped face, chin bending forward, groove-shaped eyes and mouth. The inner wall of the central hole was polished smooth. The shape of this Cong is obviously influenced by Liangzhu culture, but the level of technology is lower.

3.61 七孔刀（北阴阳营文化）（图 3.61）

长 44.5 cm，宽 13.7 cm，刀背厚 0.8 cm，刃厚 0.1 cm，重 1300 g。

碧玉，有黑色斑纹，鸡骨白沁色，玉声似磬，蜡状光泽。

此刀自刀背至刀刃均匀减薄，纵断面呈楔形，刀刃呈凸弧形，刀背略上弯。近刀背边缘均匀分布七个对钻孔，孔间距为 4.5 cm。刀之两侧外斜。此刀造型规整，制作精致，磨光度好。它与一件北阴阳营文化石刀形似，故知其为相同的文化遗物。

图 3.61　七孔刀（北阴阳营文化）

Figure 3.61　Seven-hole knife（Beiyinyangying culture）

3.61 Seven-hole Knife（Beiyinyangying Culture）（Figure 3.61）

Length: 44.5 cm, width: 13.7 cm, maximum thickness: 0.8 cm, blade thickness: 0.1 cm, weight: 1300 g.

It is made of jasper with corrosive black and chicken bone-white markings, waxy luster and wonderful percussion.

The knife is uniform thinning from the upper edge to the blade. Its shape is convex arc-shaped blade, and the upper edge slightly convex and oblique side edges. There are seven drilling holes evenly distributed by the upper edge, and the hole-span is 4.5 cm. The knife has well balance, exquisite techniques and good polishing. It is similar to the stone knife unearthed from Beiyinyangying site, so we know that they're the relics of the same archaeological culture.

3.62 舌形玉斧（江淮地区原始文化）（图 3.62）

长 13.6 cm，宽 10～10.8 cm，厚 0.9～2.5 cm，重 920 g。

青玉，灰色沁色，灰皮厚重，多蚀斑、蚀孔、蜡状光泽。

斧呈舌形，刃部较宽，肩部较窄。自肩部至刃部均匀减薄，纵断面略呈楔形。肩部平直，刃呈凸弧形。近肩部中央有一对钻孔，孔内有台阶。斧表面有磨制痕迹。此斧造型规整，磨制光滑。

1952 年，江苏淮安青莲岗文化遗址曾出土一件与此件形似的石斧，故知此斧属江淮地区原始文化玉器。

3.62 Tongue-shaped Ax（Jianghuai Primitive Culture）（Figure 3.62）

Length: 13.6 cm, width: 10—10.8 cm, thickness: 0.9—2.5 cm, weight: 920 g.

It is made of sapphire with corrosive gray skin, pits and spots, and waxy luster.

It is a tongue-shaped ax, and the blade is wider than the shoulder. It is thinned evenly from the shoulder to the blade; its vertical-section is in wedge shape. The shoulder is flat and straight, and the blade is in convex curve shape. There is a bifacial drilling hole at the middle near the shoulder, and a step on the wall of the hole. This jade ax is well-balanced with good polishing.

A similar stone ax was unearthed from the Qingliangang cultural site, Huai'an County, Jiangsu Province in 1952, so this jade ax should belong to Jianghuai primitive cultural jade work.

图 3.62 舌形玉斧（江淮地区原始文化）

Figure 3.62 Tongue-shaped ax（Jianghuai primitive culture）

3.63 腰鼓形珠串(龙山文化)(图 3.63)

此珠串由 24 粒腰鼓形玉珠组成。它们的玉质、造型与工艺皆相同,尺寸相近。玉珠间以小木珠相间。

长 2 ~ 2.2 cm,腰部直径 1.4 ~ 1.5 cm,端面直径 0.8 ~ 1 cm。

青玉,质优,棕色沁色,有灰皮,蜡状光泽。

玉珠呈腰鼓形,端面平齐。中间有一对钻直孔。此珠串造型规整,磨光度好,属新石器时期玉器之佳作。

这类玉珠始见于泛红山文化。新石器时期,大汶口文化、良渚文化皆有这类玉珠。总体观之,此珠串可能属于大汶口文化玉器或稍晚的龙山文化玉器。

3.63 Drum-shaped Beads （Longshan Culture）(Figure 3.63)

The string of beads included 24 pieces of drum-shaped beads, whose material, shape and technique process are same and with similar size. The jade bead alternated between two small wooden beads in the string. Their dimensions are as follows:

Length: 2—2.2 cm, waist diameter: 1.4—1.5 cm, ends diameter: 0.8—1 cm.

They are made of sapphire with corrosive brown markings and waxy luster.

These beads are in drum shape with flat ends, and there is a straight central drilling hole on each bead. These beads are in neat shape and good polishing, and they are the excellent work of the Neolithic period.

This kind of beads first appeared in Pan-Hongshan cultural jade. During the Neolithic period, the drum-shaped beads were found in Dawenkou and Liangzhu cultural districts. These beads maybe belong to Dawenkou or later Longshan cultural jade works.

图 3.63　腰鼓形珠串(龙山文化)

Figure 3.63　Drum-shaped beads
(Longshan culture)

3.64 管状玉珠串（龙山文化）（图 3.64）

此珠串由 18 粒圆管形玉珠组成。它们的玉质、造型与工艺均相同，尺寸相近。玉珠间以小玻璃珠相间。

长 2.8~3 cm，直径 0.7~0.8 cm。

青玉，棕色沁色，有灰皮、蚀斑及蚀孔。

珠呈圆管形，由方柱形管状珠磨去棱角而制成，其中有些珠尚有棱痕。每一珠两端面间有一对钻直孔。从造型与工艺观之，此珠串属龙山文化玉作。

图 3.64　管状玉珠串（龙山文化）

Figure 3.64　Tubular jade beads（Longshan culture）

3.64　Tubular Jade Beads（Longshan Culture）（Figure 3.64）

This string of beads consists of 18 pieces of tubular jade beads. Their material, shape and technique process are same and with similar size, and the jade bead alternated between two small glass beads in the string. Their dimensions are as follows:

Length: 2.8—3 cm, diameter: 0.7—0.8 cm.

They are made of sapphire with corrosive brown markings and spots.

They are in cylindrical tube shape. The processing is to make a square column tube and then rub off the corners to form into cylindrical shape. The trace of the processing is still left on the surface of the beads. Each of the beads was drilled a straight central hole. These beads are the relics of Longshan culture.

3.65 弹头形珠（龙山文化）（图 3.65）

高 2.5 cm，宽 1.5 cm，厚 1.2 cm。

青玉，棕、黑沁色，蜡状光泽。

珠形似弹头，横断面呈椭圆形，中间有一纵向直孔。表面饰兽面纹，其形为双目圆凸，张大口，牙齿以斜方格纹饰之，兽目上方有两道阴刻弦纹，其间饰阴刻斜线纹。类似形状的玉珠曾发现于江苏新沂花厅，属大汶口文化玉作。但从工艺看，此珠应属新石器时期晚期玉器，因为已使用铊机，可能是龙山文化晚期玉作。

3.65 Bullet-shaped Bead（Longshan Culture）（Figure 3.65）

Height: 2.5 cm, width: 1.5 cm, thickness: 1.2 cm.

It is made of sapphire with corrosive brown and black markings, and waxy luster.

The bead is in bullet shape with a central straight hole, and the cross-section is in oval shape. An animal mask was decorated on the surface. Its shape is round convex eyes, opened mouth and grinning teeth. The teeth are decorated with oblique grids, with a circular band above the eyes and decorated with incised diagonal lines. The similar beads have been found in Huating site, Xinyi City, Jiangsu Province, which belongs to Dawenkou cultural relic. But the rolling machine had been used in this bead processing, so it should be the late Longshan cultural jade work.

图 3.65 弹头形珠（龙山文化）

Figure 3.65 Bullet-shaped bead (Longshan culture)

3.66　女子立像（凌家滩文化）（图 3.66）

高 9.3 cm，宽 2.8 cm，厚 1.2 cm。

青玉，棕、红沁色，有灰皮。

女子呈直立状，头型较圆，枣核形双目高凸，眼角略上挑，直鼻，"一"字形口，纹饰皆以浮雕饰出。头上发型为一蝴蝶结。双乳及腹部隆起，双手相握置于腹前。腰臂间左右各有一圆孔。双腿直立，双足并拢，两小腿间有一椭圆形长孔。背面沿纵向打洼呈凹面。颈后有一对钻隧孔。

此玉女的制作具有红山文化玉作的特点，即以浮雕与磨制为主，工艺难度较高。其造型比例适度，突现了女性的特点，是难得的史前人物玉作。若将此玉女与凌家滩出土的玉男比较，可以看出，它们的造型与神韵相似，特别是五官（参看《中国玉器全集1》图 58）。所以此作品是融合南北风格的玉作。我们称它是凌家滩文化型玉器，因为它可能是凌家滩文化的早期作品。

3.66　Woman Statue（Lingjiatan Culture）（Figure 3.66）

Height: 9.3 cm, width: 2.8 cm, thickness: 1.2 cm.

It is made of sapphire with corrosive brownish red markings and gray spots.

The woman is in upright standing attitude, whose shape is round head, convex date kernel-shaped eyes sloping up, straight nose, closed mouth. The motifs are decorated with bas-relief technique, butterfly node-shaped hair style, plump breasts and bulged abdomen. The hands held together and placed on the abdomen. There is a pair of drilling holes between elbow and waist on both sides, straight legs, feet closed together, a long oval-shaped hole between the two legs, and concave back. There is a drilling hole on the back of her neck.

The production process of this woman statue has the characteristics of the Pan-Hongshan cultural jade works, which means that the relief and grinding techniques are the main process. The shape of the statue is in appropriate proportion, and highlights the characteristics of the woman, so it is a rare jade work of the prehistoric human statues. Comparing this woman statue with the man statue unearthed from Lingjiatan site, it can be seen that their shape, demeanor, especially their facial features are similar (see *The Complete Works of Chinese Jade, Volume 1*, Figure 58). Therefore, this jade work is the integration of the north and south jade styles. We temporary call it Lingjiatan cultural jade, and it may be the early work of Lingjiatan culture.

图 3.66　女子立像
（凌家滩文化）
**Figure 3.66　Woman statue
(Lingjiatan culture)**

3.67 立姿人像（卑南文化）（图 3.67）

高 25 cm，宽 8.5 cm，厚 1.4 cm。

青玉，棕色沁色，有灰皮、蚀斑及蚀孔。

这是一件片状镂空双面雕立姿男子，玉人双手叉腰，双臂与上体间有镂空腰圆形孔，双足外撇，双腿间镂空呈"O"形。头呈圆环形，头顶有狗图腾标志，狗仰首，翘尾，双目圆凸，双耳直立。玉人的颈、肘与膝部均饰沟槽纹。边缘皆磨制成圆角。此玉人与台湾台东县卑南遗址出土玉人形似，属卑南文化型玉器（参看《中国玉器全集 1》图 301）。这种造型的人物玉饰源自泛红山文化时期，是畎夷即犬封氏人物造像。《红山文化玉记》图 1.26 即是一件泛红山文化同类的玉作，外形与这件相似，是一个女性的造型。

3.67 A Human Statue（Beinan Culture）（Figure 3.67）

Height: 25 cm, width: 8.5 cm, thickness: 1.4 cm.

It is made of sapphire with corrosive brown markings and spots.

It is a flaky hollow man's statue. Its shape is standing posture with akimbo arms, splayed feet, O-shaped legs, ring-shaped head with a dog totemic symbol on the top. The shape of the dog is looking up, tail bending upward, convex round eyes, ears upright. The groove patterns were decorated on the man's neck, elbow and knee. The edges were grinded smooth. This statue is similar to the jade human statue unearthed from the Beinan site, Taiwan（see *The Complete Works of Chinese Jade, Volume 1*, Figure 301）. This kind of human statue originated from Pan-Hongshan cultural period. It is the statue of Quanfeng Clan, and the human statue showed in Figure 1.26 in *The Hongshan Cultural Jade Record* is the Quanfeng's human statue of Pan-Hongshan culture which is similar to this one, but is a woman statue.

图 3.67 立姿人像（卑南文化型）

Figure 3.67 A human statue (Beinan culture)

3.68 戚（二里头文化）（图 3.68）

高 5.6 cm，宽 6 cm，最厚 1.5 cm，中央孔径 1.2 cm。

青玉，棕、红沁色，有灰皮、蚀斑及蚀孔。

此戚的外缘呈曲边七边形，刃部由四段凹弧连成。肩呈凸弧形，两侧外斜，其上饰两组减地凸脊，每一凸脊上有三齿。顶端有一对钻小孔。戚身中间有一大孔。器身中间厚，内外边缘均减薄，横断面呈梭形。锋刃很薄。此戚造型美观，工艺精湛。二里头文化遗址曾出土类似的玉戚，此器型延续到商代（参看《中国玉器全集 2》图 11）。此器具有泛红山文化玉器的制作风格，工艺难度较高。

3.68 Qi Pendant（Erlitou Culture）（Figure 3.68）

Height: 5.6 cm, width: 6 cm, maximum thickness: 1.5 cm, aperture of central hole: 1.2 cm.

It is made of sapphire with corrosive brownish red markings, spots and pits.

The contour of the Qi is in curved heptagon shape. The blade is formed by four connected concaved arc segments. The shoulder is in convex arc shape, and the side edges are oblique. Two ridges are decorated on each side edge, and each ridge with three teeth. A small hole was drilled on the top. There is a funnel-shaped big hole on the middle of its body. The periphery of the Qi was chamfered, and the blade is very thin. This Qi is in beautiful appearance with exquisite workmanship. The similar Qi pieces had been unearthed from Erlitou site, and this type of Qi had been extending to the Shang Dynasty（see *The Complete Works of Chinese Jade, Volume 2*, Figure 11）. This jade Qi has the Pan-Hongshan cultural jade style, whose technological process is very difficult.

图 3.68 戚（二里头文化）

Figure 3.68 Qi pendant (Erlitou culture)

3.69　璋（二里头文化）（图 3.69）

长 19.6 cm，锋端宽 5.1 cm，手柄宽 3 cm，厚 1 cm。

青玉，棕、红沁色，有灰皮、蚀斑及蚀纹。

璋自格部至锋端逐渐变宽，锋端呈斜凹弧形。格部两侧各有两个并列方形凸脊，每一凸脊上饰有两个齿牙。手柄近格部中间有一圆孔，孔内壁有台阶。

玉璋源自泛红山文化时期，流行于新石器时期晚期至商周时期。它是《周礼》中所讲的六瑞之一，是礼南方之器，同时也是兵符，兼有"祀"与"戎"的双重作用。新石器时期晚期已从氏族公社转向中央集权的国家形态，已出现了军队，故玉璋的制作较多，多见于二里头文化、陕西龙山文化以及广汉文化。

图 3.69　璋（二里头文化）

Figure 3.69　Zhang（Erlitou culture）

3.69　Zhang（Erlitou Culture）（Figure 3.69）

Length: 19.6 cm, blade width: 5.1 cm, handle width: 3 cm, thickness: 1 cm.

It is made of sapphire with corrosive brownish red markings and spots.

The body of the Zhang is getting wider from the Ge to the front, and the front edge is in inclined concave arc shape. The Ge is formed by two ridges on each side, and each ridge with two teeth. There is a drilling hole on the handle and drilling marks on the wall of the hole.

Jade Zhang was originated from the Pan-Hongshan cultural period and popularized in the late Neolithic period and the Shang and Zhou Dynasties. It is the important ritual device and war symbol. During the late Neolithic period, the clan community had turned to the stage of power centralized, and the military had emerged, so jade Zhang was made more than before, and it was more prevalent in the Erlitou cultural district, Shaanxi Longshan cultural district and Guanghan cultural district.

3.70　玉铲（齐家文化）（图 3.70）

图中的两玉铲玉质、沁色、造型与工艺相同,尺寸相近。右铲刃部呈凸弧形,左铲刃部平直,尖端有残。

右:高 13.5 cm,刃宽 4.8 cm,肩宽 3.9 cm,厚 1.8 cm。

左:高 14 cm,刃宽 5.5 cm,肩宽 4.8 cm,厚 1.2 cm。

黑绿色青玉,质优,有黑色斑纹,棕色沁色,蜡状光泽,玉声清脆。

铲之轮廓呈梯形,肩部两侧均磨制成圆角。刃端单面倒角,锋刃较利。近肩部中央有一对钻孔,孔内有台阶。铲之开片均匀,造型规整,磨制光滑,属同类玉铲之精品。从玉料及制作工艺看,此玉铲当属新石器时期晚期甘青地区的齐家文化玉器。这种黑绿色玉产于甘肃临夏和酒泉等地。

图 3.70　玉铲（齐家文化）

Figure 3.70　Jade shovels (Qijia culture)

3.70　Jade Shovels（Qijia Culture）（Figure 3.70）

These two jade shovels are in the same jade, corrosive color, shape and technical process, and with similar size. The blade of the right one is in convex curved shape, and the left one with flat blade and a little bit broken on the tip. The jade and size are as follows:

（1）Right one
Height: 13.5 cm, blade width: 4.8 cm, shoulder width: 3.9 cm, thickness: 1.8 cm.

（2）Left one
Height: 14 cm, blade width: 5.5 cm, shoulder width: 4.8 cm, thickness: 1.2 cm.

They are made of black-green jade with corrosive black and brown markings, waxy luster and crisp percussion.

The contour is in trapezoidal shape, flat shoulder with smoothed corners. The blade is single-side bevel and sharp. There is a bifacial drilling hole on the middle near the shoulder, and the drilling marks were left on the wall of the hole. These shovels are well-balanced with uniform thickness and good polishing.They are high-level jade shovels. From the material and production process of view, they should belong to the Qijia cultural jade during the late Neolithic period. The black-green jade was produced in Linxia and Jiuquan cities, Gansu Province.

3.71 斧(仰韶文化)(图 3.71)

高 8.2 cm，顶端宽 5.2 cm，刃宽 8.2 cm，孔径 3.1 cm，最厚 1 cm。

全沁呈棕、黑沁色，原玉质不辨，蜡状光泽。

斧之外形呈弧边梯形，中间有一大圆孔，可称为环形斧。其顶端略有弧凸，刃端呈凸弧形。斧自顶端至刃端逐渐减薄，纵断面呈"V"形。斧之周边均磨制成圆角。孔之内壁光滑，磨去了钻痕。斧之表面尚留有开片时的割痕。此斧制作古朴，造型美观，磨制精细。河南庙底沟仰韶文化遗址出土过类似的环形玉斧，故此斧应属仰韶文化玉器。

3.71 Jade Ax (Yangshao Culture) (Figure 3.71)

Height: 8.2 cm, shoulder width: 5.2 cm, blade width: 8.2 cm, maximum thickness: 1 cm, aperture: 3.1 cm.

It was covered by corrosive brown and black skin, and waxy luster. The original jade cannot be seen.

The contour is in trapezoidal shape with a big round hole on the middle, and it can be said ring-shaped ax. Both of the blade and the shoulder are in convex arc shape. The body is uniformly getting thinner from the shoulder to the blade, and the vertical section is in wedge shape. The edges are grinded smooth, and the wall of the central hole is smooth and rubbed off the drilling marks. The carving marks were still left on the surfaces. The ax has ancient demeanor and beautiful shape with highly polishing. The similar ring-shaped jade ax was unearthed from Miaodigou cultural site, Henan Province. This jade ax should the relic of Yangshao culture.

图 3.71 斧(仰韶文化)
Figure 3.71 Jade ax (Yangshao culture)

图 3.72　有肩玉钺（仰韶文化）

Figure 3.72　Shouldered Yue (Yangshao culture)

3.72　有肩玉钺（仰韶文化）（图 3.72）

高 9.6 cm，刃宽 8.2 cm，肩宽 4.2 cm，最厚 0.7 cm。

青玉，质优，棕色沁色，有灰皮、蚀斑及蚀纹。

钺之外形为一半圆与一弧边梯形的组合，半圆部分称为"援"，梯形部分称为"内"，交接处两侧的台阶称为"肩"，援前端弧形为"刃"。此钺刃部呈半圆形，末端略有弧凸。内中央有一对钻圆孔。此钺自上端至刃端均匀减薄，刃呈钝刃形。在河南郏县裴李岗文化遗址及河北矾山镇轩辕城遗址均有这类石钺出土，故此钺应属仰韶文化玉器。

3.72　Shouldered Yue（Yangshao Culture）（Figure 3.72）

Height: 9.6 cm, blade width: 8.2 cm, shoulder width: 4.2 cm, maximum thickness: 0.7 cm.

It is made of high-quality sapphire with corrosive brown markings and spots.

The contour of the Yue is in a combinative shape of a semicircle and a trapezoid. The semi-circular part is called "Yuan", and the trapezoidal part is called "Nei". The steps on both sides of the junction are known as "shoulder", and the front of the Yuan is "blade". The blade is in semi-circular shape; there is a drilling hole on the middle of the "Nei", which is drilled from both sides. The body is uniformly getting thinner from the upper edge to the blade, and the blade is blunt. The similar stone Yue pieces were unearthed from Peiligang site, Jia County, Henan Province, and Xuanyuancheng site, Fanshan County, Hebei Province. So this Yue belongs to Yangshao cultural jade work.

参考文献
References

1.杨天佑.万古奇珍——泛红山文化玉群.杭州：浙江大学出版社,2006.

2.倪泰一,编译.山海经.昆明：云南科技出版社,1994.

3.瞿林东.中华文明史(第一卷).石家庄：河北教育出版社,1999.

4.辽宁省文物考古研究所.牛河梁红山文化遗址与玉器精粹.北京：文物出版社,1997.

5.杨伯达.中国玉器全集(第一集).石家庄：河北美术出版社,1992.

6.王大有.图说中国图腾.北京：人民美术出版社,1998.

7.杨天佑.巴蜀玉缘.杭州：浙江大学出版社,2008.

8.贝金特.文明的疑踪.苗晨,宋航,译.北京：光明日报出版社,2000.

9.侯书森.古老的密码.北京：中国城市出版社,1999.

10. 裴蓉.真实的梦幻.北京：中国城市出版社,1998.

11.徐钦奇,谢飞,王建.史前考古学新进展.北京：科学出版社,1999.

12.道金斯.伊甸园之河.王直华,译.上海：上海科学技术出版社,1997.

13.高小刚.图腾柱下.北京：三联书店,1997.

14.恺杰.人类未解之谜.北京：时事出版社,2002.

15.曹贤香.复活的古城.北京：宗教文化出版社,1999.

16.石仁.追寻文明的脚印.上海：华东师范大学出版社,1999.

17.梅森.美洲古文明.许琼莹,译.台北：时报文化出版企业股份有限公司,2003.

18.中国科学院考古研究所.考古精华.北京：科学出版社,1993.

19.段万翰.世界五千年(第1集).上海：少年儿童出版社,1990.

20.杨泓,李力.华夏之美——中国艺术图鉴.香港：中华书局,1993.

21. 李可染.中国美术全集(第1集).北京：人民美术出版社,1988.

22.中国收藏家协会.泛红山文化——中国神秘的黑皮玉雕.北京：万国学术出版社,2009.

23. 姚政.史海遗珍.香港：中华博物院出版社,2015.

24.四川大学历史系古文字研究室.甲骨金文字典.成都：巴蜀书社,1993.

后　　记

　　古玉是与中华文明密切相关的文物，世界上仅中国有一部自末次冰期至今的连续万年以上的玉器制作史。如此众多的玉器展示了各个历史时期重要的文化信息，形成了一部玉制的中华文明史。在没有文字记载的史前时期，古玉尤其凸显了其重要性，这是其他文物所不可比拟的，它们不仅是重要的中华文化遗产，也是重要的世界文化遗产。

　　笔者有幸见到自万年前至今的如此众多的玉器，这的确是难得的机会、缘分和享受，更是天赋之责。因此必须尽心竭力，奋力探索和发现，以弘扬中华玉文化、回馈世人。本人有志将撰写有 15000 年历史的中华玉文化史作为毕生的追求。本人有关中华玉文化史的第一部著作是《万古奇珍——泛红山文化玉群》，它记录了中华祖先在万年前的末次冰期晚期所创建的文明，其时间大约是距今 15000 年至 11000 年。该文明在末次冰期结束时遭到毁灭，但很多文明因素延续到新石器时期。所以新石器时期不是中华文明的开端，而是承前启后新一轮文明的开创期，在世界范围内也是如此。本系列丛书《中华新石器时期玉器丛书》记录了距今约 10000 年至 4000 年的中华新石器时期的玉文化史，依照历史年表的顺序，本书是记录中华玉文化的第二部著作，其中记录的玉器充分证实了笔者对新石器时期的论断，即新石器时期的文明是其前期文明的继承和发展，新石器时期是新一轮文明的再创期。同时证实了泛红山文化既是中华玉文化的源头，也是中华文明的重要源头。

　　令笔者感到十分欣慰的是在本书的撰写过程中得到了家人和许多友人的支持和帮助，如我的母亲袁绍英，我的老师汪浩教授、戴遗山教授，我的好友姚庭宝教授、缪鸿兴教授，著名历史学家何光岳先生，他们都给予本人很多鼓励和帮助。特别是我的学生和好友程龙保先生亲自参与了本书的编辑、资料整理和汇编、联系出版等工作。另外，特别值得一提的是韩国学者金喜镛先生，他为本书提供了有关黑皮玉的实地考察资料和一部分刻有文字的黑皮玉；著名黑皮玉收藏家董剑女士，她为本书提供了黑皮玉玉屏和玉册的照片。对于他们的帮助，在此一并深表谢意。

Postscript

The ancient jade works are cultural relics closely associated with Chinese civilization. Only China has the consecutive jade production history which has more than ten thousand years since the Last Glacial. So many jade works have showed the important cultural information of each historical period, and formed of a jade history of Chinese civilization. In the absence of written records of prehistoric times, ancient jade works were in particular highlighting their importance, which is unmatched by other cultural relics. They are not only an important Chinese cultural heritage, but also an important world cultural heritage.

I had the honor to see so many jades from ten thousand years ago to the present, which is indeed a rare chance, fate and enjoy, and the responsibility given by God. For this, I have to work hard to explore, discover and create, in order to promote Chinese jade culture, and contribute back to the people. I have a will to write the fifteen thousand years of Chinese jade culture history as a lifelong pursuit. My first book about the Chinese jade cultural history is the book *The Earliest Miraculous Treasures—Pan-Hongshan Cultural Jade Group*, which recorded the Chinese ancestors created civilization in the late Last Glacial, and it is dating back to about fifteen to eleven thousand years ago. This civilization was destroyed at the end of the Last Glacial, but many civilized factors continued to the Neolithic period. So the Neolithic period is not the beginning period of the Chinese civilization, but the period of continuation and development of its former civilization, and also a creating period of a new round human civilization, and the situation is the same in the world. The series of books *The Series of Neolithic Jade Recordes of China* and recorded the Chinese Neolithic jade culture history, which is about from ten thousand years ago to four thousand years ago. In chronological order, the series is the second book recording the Chinese jade culture, whose records of jade works in this series fully confirmed the author's judgment on the Neolithic period. I.e., Neolithic civilization is the inheritance and development of its former civilization, and the Neolithic period is the creating period of another new round of civilization. As well it confirmed that Pan-Hongshan culture is the original source of Chinese jade culture, also an important source of Chinese civilization.

I am very pleased to get lots of support and help from my family and friends in the process of writing the book, such as my mother Yuan Shaoying, my teacher Professor Wang Hao, Professor Dai Yishan, my good friend Professor Yao Tingbao, Professor Miao Hongxing, the famous historian Mr. He Guangyue. They have given me a lot of encouragement and help. Especially my student and good friend Mr. Cheng Longbao was personally involved in the editing, data compilation and assembly of the book, publishing contact and so on. In addition, what particularly worth mentioning is that the Korean scholar Mr. Kim Hee-Yong, who provided fieldwork information about the black-shell jade and a portion of black-shell jade works on which there are carved writing characters for this book; and the famous black-shell jade collector Ms. Dong Jian, who provided some photos of the black-shell jade painted screens and jade books for this book. Here I would like to express my heartfelt thanks to them for their help.